SCHOLASTIC

READ&RESPOND

Bringing the best books to life in the classroom

Guided Reading

Key Stage 1

Comprehensive guided reading notes for:

- Oliver's Vegetables
- Stick Man
- Aliens Love Underpants
- Room on the Broom
- The Lighthouse Keeper's Lunch
- Winnie the Witch

AGES
6–7

Scholastic Education, an imprint of Scholastic Ltd
Book End, Range Road, Witney, Oxfordshire, OX29 0YD
Registered office: Westfield Road, Southam, Warwickshire CV47 0RA
www.scholastic.co.uk
© 2017, Scholastic Ltd
1 2 3 4 5 6 7 8 9   7 8 9 0 1 2 3 4 5 6

British Library Cataloguing-in-Publication Data
A catalogue record for this book is available from the British Library.
ISBN 978-1407-16946-0
Printed and bound by Ashford Colour Press

Due to the nature of the web we cannot guarantee the content or links of any site mentioned. We strongly recommend that teachers check websites before using them in the classroom.

Every effort has been made to trace copyright holders for the works reproduced in this book, and the publishers apologise for any inadvertent omissions.

Extracts from National Curriculum for England, English Programme of Study © Crown Copyright. Reproduced under the terms of the Open Government Licence (OGL). www.nationalarchives.gov.uk/doc/open-government-licence/version/3/

Authors Jean Evans, Samantha Pope, Sarah Snashall
Editorial Rachel Morgan, Jenny Wilcox, Kate Buckley, Niamh O'Carroll, Elizabeth Evans
Cover and Series Design Neil Salt and Nicolle Thomas
Layout Neil Salt

CONTENTS

▼ INTRODUCTION

Read & Respond provides teaching ideas related to a specific children's book. The series focuses on best-loved books and brings you ways to use them to engage your class and enthuse them about reading. This book provides detailed guided reading sessions for six children's books.

GUIDED READING

Guided reading is usually conducted in small groups with children of a similar reading ability, under teacher guidance. The groups are often around six to eight children, although may be fewer depending on the children in your class. The sessions are likely to be short, around 20 minutes, and focused on reading and comprehension skills.

There should be one focus text and each child should have a copy of it. The text should be slightly more challenging than the children's independent reading level, where they can read and understand the vast majority of the text independently. The teacher facilitation of guided reading allows for the children to access more challenging materials in a supported environment – they should still be able to understand and access 90 per cent of the content though.

Guided reading is much more than just reading in turns. Time should be given for reading independently; the teacher may wish to listen to individual children, but this should be followed up by checking the children's understanding and comprehension of the text through discussion and questioning.

How this book relates to the *Read & Respond* teacher's book

This book can be used for stand-alone sessions or in conjunction with the corresponding *Read & Respond* teacher's books. Each *Read & Respond* teacher's book is designed for whole-class teaching and contains a variety of activities that look at grammar, punctuation, phonics and spelling; plot, character and setting; speaking and listening; and writing.

While there are guided reading notes in the teacher's book, the ones provided in this book are much more detailed and therefore the two books can work together. If you are using a carousel system for guided reading, then the teacher's book may provide supporting activities to use when the children are not in the guided reading group. Within this book, there may be some optional links referenced to the *Read & Respond* teacher's book, where work could be expanded.

ABOUT THE BOOK

Each children's book has been divided into four guided reading sessions. The sessions work through each book progressively, so you read it over a number of weeks. It has been assumed that the sessions will be conducted in guided reading groups of around six to eight children; if you plan to use them differently, then they can be adapted accordingly. Each session follows a similar structure:

Session aims: The purpose of the session and what children will be focused on in their reading.

Before the session: If there is anything the children need to do prior to the session, such as reading some of the book, this will be identified here.

Read: This section will focus on the children reading the text either independently or as a group. It may be reading new chapters or sections of the book or re-reading parts of the book that they have read previously. They should consider questions about the text while reading and then discuss these as a group to check their understanding.

Revisit and respond: A range of different activities will have been provided under this heading to provide flexibility to select appropriate tasks for the group. As each session is only intended to be around 20 minutes long, it is advised that one or two of these activity ideas are used to meet the needs of your children.

Assessment opportunities: A bank of questions has been provided which could be used at any point in the session as relevant. They are sub-divided into headings to identify the purpose of the type of question.

At the end of the book, you will find two templates that you can use to support your guided reading sessions:

Guided Reading Bookmark Template: This template provides a bookmark that you can complete and give to the children as reference. It could include the questions you want them to consider when reading or you could use the assessment opportunities questions for the children to discuss.

Guided Reading Record Template: A template to record any notes from a guided reading session so you have a record that you can refer to.

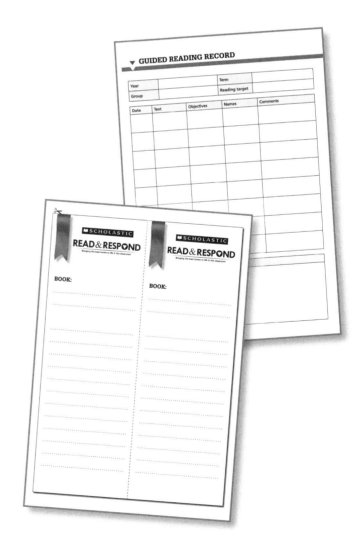

▼ SESSION 1: OFF TO GRANDPA'S

SESSION AIMS

Making predictions; focusing on the main characters and the story set-up.

READ

- Open the book out flat and look at the image that goes across the front and back cover. Read the blurb with the children and ask them to decide who the characters are in the illustration.

- Ask:
  - What's Oliver holding out in his hand?
  - Have you ever seen carrots with the leaves on?
  - How do carrots grow?
  - What else can we see in the illustration?
  - What vegetables do you like to eat?

- Establish that we can see Grandpa's impressive vegetable patch behind Oliver in the cover image. Talk about what the children know about how different vegetables grow.

- Read the opening three spreads (up to '…"Is it a bargain?"'). Check the children's understanding by asking the following questions:
  - Where is Oliver going?
  - How is he getting there?
  - What does Oliver think is the best thing about Grandpa's house?
  - What vegetables does Oliver like to eat?
  - What is the deal that Oliver strikes with Grandpa?

- Revisit these first three spreads, asking volunteers to read the story aloud, using correct intonation and indicating when people are talking.

During reading

- Move around the group and 'tune in' to hear individuals read aloud. Encourage and praise good expression.

REVISIT AND RESPOND

Bring the group back together and discuss some of the points below to help the children think about the cover and the first three spreads in more depth.

Note: Since there are only 20 minutes for each session, you are advised to focus on only one or two of the elements that are listed below.

- Ask: *What sort of person do you think Oliver is? What have we found out about him so far?* Challenge pairs to come up with three facts about Oliver – one from each spread. Share the children's ideas, agreeing that we know that Oliver likes to walk places, that he thinks Grandpa's garden is wonderful and that it's his favourite thing about Grandpa's house, and we know that the only vegetable he likes to eat is potatoes cooked as chips. Ask: *Do you think Oliver is going to keep his bargain? If so, do you think he is going to like the vegetables he eats?*

- Talk about the character of Grandpa. Ask: *What is Grandpa like? Can we find any clues in the story so far?* Ask the children to discuss ideas in pairs before sharing their thoughts. Agree that we know that Grandpa is proud of growing his own vegetables. Help the children to make the link between how Grandpa talks – *proudly* – and how he feels. Ask: *Can we also infer that Grandpa loves his garden and growing vegetables?* Suggest that it is a lot of work to grow your own vegetables and it is unlikely he would do it if he didn't love it.

- Focus on the illustration on the second spread. Ask for some suggestions as to what vegetables might be growing here. Some children might spot some peas if they've seen a pea plant growing, or the pumpkin and the carrots. Allow time for them to talk about the vegetables they eat and how they are prepared.

- Explain to the children that Oliver is going to spend a week with his grandparents. Ask: *How do you think he feels about this? How does he look in the illustrations? What might he miss? What will he enjoy? Why do you think he's staying with his grandparents?* (Explain that there's no way of knowing, but perhaps he is on his school holidays and his mother still needs to work.) *Have you ever stayed away from home on your own?* Allow time for the children to discuss times that they've been away from home. Encourage them to talk about how they felt. Talk about what we might miss when we go away – for example, our family, our toys, our bedroom, familiar food, and so on. Talk about what is exciting about going away – for example, new places, being made a fuss of, day trips to interesting places, and so on.

- Re-read the third spread. Ask the children to help you work out what a 'bargain' is and what 'no complaints' mean. Allow time for them to discuss the meaning together before clarifying. Ask the children to look at the picture of Oliver and Grandpa shaking hands. Ask: *Why are Grandpa and Oliver shaking hands here? Is it to say hello?* Agree that this is Oliver and Grandpa shaking on their deal.

Ask the children, whenever appropriate, to revisit the text to exemplify/support the answers.

Encourage the children to read aloud back to the group when referring back to the text – praise clear, confident and expressive reading.

ASSESSMENT OPPORTUNITIES

The following bank of question prompts provides a quick and easy means of monitoring the children's comprehension skills and understanding of the text. The children's answers to a question must be supported by evidence from the text.

Understanding
- What vegetable is Oliver shown holding on the cover?
- What does Oliver like to eat?
- How does Oliver want to travel to his grandparents?
- What vegetable does Oliver leave on his plate at lunchtime?
- What does Oliver like most about his grandparents' house?
- What is the deal that Oliver makes with Grandpa?

Inferences
- Does Oliver know how potatoes grow? How do you know?
- Why does Oliver want to walk to his grandparents'?
- Does Grandpa like gardening?

Predicting
- Do you think Oliver will try all the vegetables he finds?
- Will Oliver like any of the vegetables he finds?

Main ideas
- What are the main events of the opening of the story?

Language, structure and presentation
- What does it mean to make a bargain with someone?
- Can you say the sentence, 'If you find something else, you eat that and no complaints' in your own words?

Themes and conventions
- Do you think Oliver is a healthy boy?

SESSION 2: ON MONDAY

SESSION AIMS

Focusing on the development of the main character, and the setting.

READ

- Open out the cover of *Oliver's Vegetables* again and ask the children to tell you the story so far. Refresh their memories by asking the following:
  - Who are the two people on the back cover of the book?
  - What is Oliver holding in his hand?
  - What does Oliver like to eat?
  - What bargain does Oliver strike with Grandpa?
- Ask the children to read the next three spreads (4 to 6) independently. Listen in to individual children, praising confident expression and encouraging them to try to decipher the meaning of unfamiliar vocabulary.

During reading

- Move around the group and 'tune in' to hear individuals read aloud. Encourage and praise good expression.

REVISIT AND RESPOND

Bring the group back together and discuss some of the points below to help the children think about spreads 4 to 6 in more depth.

Note: Since there are only 20 minutes for each session, you are advised to focus on only one or two of the elements that are listed below.

- Re-read spread 4 up to '"Carrots," said Grandpa.' Ask: *Is Oliver going to keep his side of the bargain? Is he going to eat the carrots?* Remind the children that, in the past, Oliver has only ever eaten chips. Ask: *Do you think that his mother has ever suggested that he tries carrots or other vegetables?* Point out the peas left on his plate on the first spread. Continue to read the rest of the page and discuss any surprise at Oliver keeping his side of the bargain.

- Ask: *What have we learned about Oliver so far?* Gather together known and inferred information about the character: his enjoyment of the garden and being outside. Ask the children to look at spreads 4, 5 and 6 and come up with some adjectives about Oliver, finding evidence in the text. For example:
  - enthusiastic – he pulls up the nearest leaves; shouts '"HERE THEY ARE!"'; 'Oliver got up early'
  - energetic – 'Oliver ran round the garden'; he is willing to give eating vegetables a go
  - thoughtful – 'Oliver took a long time making up his mind'.

- Re-read spreads 5 and 6, helping the children to read and understand 'crinkly', 'spinach' and 'rhubarb'. Point out the word 'carrots'. Ask: *What is the ending here?* Agree that an 's' has been added to carrot to make it plural. Challenge pairs to find other plurals in the first six spreads of the book, and to decide whether 's' or 'es' has been added to make the plural. (Tell them to watch out for words that end in 'e' in the singular.) Agree that there is: vegetable + s, chip + s, complaint + s and potato + es. Ask: *What about leaves? What is the ending here?* Agree that this is an unusual word and that the singular of leaves is leaf: to make the plural, the 'f' has turned into a 'v' + 'es'.

- Ask: *Apart from plural endings, what other endings can you find in these pages? Can you say what the original (root) word was?* Challenge partners to find three words and write them down to discuss what the root word was each time and how it was spelled. Together discuss: proud + ly, hide + ing, near + est, make + ing, crinkle + ly, smile + ed, pull + ed. Ask the children to circle the words where the root word changes when the ending is added.

- As a group, come up with a list of as many story settings as you can, from books or films; for example, a castle, a forest, a pirate ship, under the sea, a racetrack, an island, and so on. Ask: *How does a back garden with a vegetable patch compare with these more exciting settings? How might it be interesting for Oliver?* Ask the children to work in pairs to compare the vegetable patch with other settings. Ask: *What makes the vegetable patch interesting?* Discuss the fact that it is an unknown place for Oliver, that he loves it and that he is on a voyage of discovery. Look at the illustrations and point out to the children that the plants are painted huge and it almost looks as if Oliver is in the rainforest.

- Talk about the wider setting of Grandpa's garden, beyond the vegetable patch. Look at the image of Oliver shaking hands with Grandpa. Ask: *What else is there in the garden? What might be in the shed? What's in the greenhouse? Do you think that Oliver is allowed to play inside the shed and greenhouse?* Tell the children to work with a partner to orally describe the inside of the shed and greenhouse. Remind them how neat Grandpa's garden and vegetable patch are: are the shed and greenhouse likely to be the same?

Ask the children, whenever appropriate, to revisit the text to exemplify/support the answers.

Encourage the children to read aloud back to the group when referring back to the text – praise clear, confident and expressive reading.

ASSESSMENT OPPORTUNITIES

The following bank of question prompts provides a quick and easy means of monitoring the children's comprehension skills and understanding of the text. The children's answers to a question must be supported by evidence from the text.

Understanding
- How do Oliver and his grandparents eat rhubarb?
- Why does Oliver think that the rhubarb is potatoes?
- What is the first vegetable Oliver finds?

Inferences
- Why can't Oliver find the potatoes?
- Do we know what Oliver thought about the carrots?
- What does the dog think about finding carrots?
- Does Oliver enjoy the vegetable game?

Predicting
- Do you think that Oliver will find a vegetable that he doesn't like?

Main ideas
- What vegetables has Oliver eaten so far?
- What does Oliver think about the vegetables he's eaten?

Language, structure and presentation
- What do you think crinkly leaves look like?
- What sort of vegetable is rhubarb?
- What is spinach?
- Add 'ing' to these words: smile, pull, make, cook. Did you have to make any changes to the root words?

Themes and conventions
- Do you think that Oliver is healthier now?

▼ SESSION 3: CRUNCHY CABBAGE

SESSION AIMS

Looking at the vocabulary used in the book and encouraging the children to generate their own descriptive phrases.

READ

- Ask the children to work together to tell the story so far. Ask them to talk about the different predictions they had in the last two sessions and which they were right about and which they weren't.
- Ask the children to read spreads 7 and 8 independently, bearing the following questions in mind:
  - What does Oliver do when it stops raining?
  - How does he go outside? (He hurries.)
  - Does this fit with what we know about Oliver? (Yes, he likes to be outside.)
  - How do you think he felt inside in the rain? (Probably frustrated – we know he likes to be outside and that he hurries out as soon as it stops raining.)
  - Where did Oliver find the beetroot?
  - What happened when he pulled at the leaves?
- Read aloud spread 9, asking the children to follow in their copies. Model using phonics knowledge to read *'tangle'* and *'delicious'* before discussing the meaning.

During reading

- Move around the group and 'tune in' to hear individuals read aloud. Encourage and praise good expression.

REVISIT AND RESPOND

Bring the group back together and discuss some of the points below to help the children think about spreads 7, 8 and 9 in more depth.

Note: Since there are only 20 minutes for each session, you are advised to focus on only one or two of the elements that are listed below.

- Point out the animals on spread 7: the dog, the slug and the snail. Ask: *How do you think Oliver feels about animals?* Explain that slugs and snails like to eat many vegetables, particularly cabbages. Explain that slugs and snails like the ground when it is moist after rain. Allow time for the children to share their knowledge of the way slugs and snails move by making a slippery track, and the silvery trails that they can leave on plants or paths. Tell pairs to find two pieces of evidence that prove that Oliver likes cabbage. (He has two helpings and says it is 'Very, very good'.)
- Focus on spread 8. Establish that beetroot, like carrots, is a root vegetable. Challenge the children to guess what the flower is behind Oliver (probably a sunflower). Write the word 'beetroot' on a small whiteboard. Ask: *What two words are used to make this word?* Challenge the children to find two more compound words in the book up to this point ('something', 'football').
- Ask the children to mime pulling up a beetroot until it pops out of the ground. Tell a version of the story 'The enormous turnip' changing it to 'The enormous beetroot' and using the children's names in height order, finishing with the smallest child. Encourage the children to join in with the repetitive parts of the story.
- Ask the children to discuss with a partner how each of the vegetables found so far grows, encouraging them to look for clues in the text or in the pictures. Fill in any missing knowledge, pointing out the part of the vegetable that is eaten

on the relevant pages. Ask the children to look at the different colours of the different vegetables. Ask: *Are all the greens the same?* Point out the red veins in the leaves of the beetroot. Ask: *Are the beetroot and the rhubarb the same colour?* As a group, write some descriptive noun phrases for the vegetables, encouraging the children to suggest different adjectives until everyone is happy with the choice; for example, sunny orange carrots with frothy leaves; bright crinkly spinach; mysterious pink rhubarb hiding under umbrella leaves; slug-infested tight-knit cabbages; deep purple, muddy beetroot.

- Look back at Oliver's plate on the first spread. Ask: *How do you think Oliver would describe carrots, peas, spinach, rhubarb, cabbage, beetroot and peas at this stage in the story?* Enjoy coming up with a range of negative describing words for vegetables (particularly badly cooked ones); for example, mushy, yucky, slimy, bitter, gritty, sour, foul, disgusting, inedible. Next, tell pairs to work together to find all the things that Oliver says and does that show what he thinks about the vegetables he eats at his grandparents' (including the number of helpings and the clean plate). Discuss as a group the way that, as he gets more enthusiastic, the number of helpings and the number of times he says 'very' increases.

- Return to the theme of healthy living. Ask the children to remember in what way Oliver was healthy at the beginning of the story. (He liked to walk and be outside.) Ask: *In what way was he not healthy? Is he healthier now? What has helped Oliver to be healthier?* (Grandpa's encouragement and his own bravery.) Explain that 'healthy living' and 'being brave' are two ideas that we find in this book.

Ask the children, whenever appropriate, to revisit the text to exemplify/support the answers.

Encourage the children to read aloud back to the group when referring back to the text – praise clear, confident and expressive reading.

ASSESSMENT OPPORTUNITIES

The following bank of question prompts provides a quick and easy means of monitoring the children's comprehension skills and understanding of the text. The children's answers to a question must be supported by evidence from the text.

Understanding
- How does beetroot grow?
- How do peas grow?
- What happens when Oliver kicks his football into the vegetable patch?
- Does Oliver like the pea soup?

Inferences
- What do you think Oliver did while it was raining?
- Why were the slugs and snails on the cabbages?
- Do you think Gran and Grandpa are good cooks?

Predicting
- What do you think Oliver's mother will say when she hears about the vegetables that Oliver has eaten?

Main ideas
- Can you name three different plant parts that we can eat?

Language, structure and presentation
- What sort of vegetable is beetroot?
- How does Oliver describe beetroot?
- What vegetable has crinkly leaves?
- What vegetable does Oliver find in a tangle of sticks and leaves?

Themes and conventions
- In what way is Oliver brave in the story so far?

▼ SESSION 4: CHIPS FOR TEA!

SESSION AIMS

Considering how the days of the week structure the story.

READ

- Recap on the story so far. Establish that Oliver has tried and enjoyed a whole range of vegetables, and talk about what might happen at the end of the story. Agree that he still needs to find the potatoes. Ask: *Do you think he'll find them?* Perhaps he'll find them but decide that chips are horrible now.

  - Ask volunteers to read the last three spreads (10 to 12) of the story. Afterwards ask:
  - How does Oliver find the potatoes?
  - What do Oliver, Gran and Grandpa do with the potatoes?
  - Why do you think the words '"HERE THEY ARE!"' are written in capitals?
  - Can you work out from the picture how potatoes grow?
  - Why did Gran and Grandpa laugh when Oliver's mother sees Oliver eating chips?

- On the last page, pause to look at the spelling of 'different', 'walked', 'stared', 'mother', 'other' and 'laughed'. As a group, unpick the spelling of each and discuss how each differs from its pronunciation.

During reading

- Talk about the meaning of unfamiliar words as they come up, encouraging the children to try to tackle them themselves.

REVISIT AND RESPOND

Bring the group back together and discuss some of the points below which relate to the whole book.

Note: Since there are only 20 minutes for each session, you are advised to focus on only one or two of the elements that are listed below.

- Ask: *What event starts the story?* Agree that it is Oliver's trip to visit his grandparents. Ask: *What is the structure of the story after that?* Help the children to see that it is structured around the days of the week, and that each day Oliver finds and eats a different vegetable. Give each pair a small whiteboard and ask them to write the days of the week in a column down the left-hand side. As they write, talk about each day of the week and its own particular tricky spelling. Help children to articulate which part of each word differs from its pronunciation. Talk about strategies for remembering these spellings; for example, pronouncing the words as they are spelled when writing them. Next, challenge the pairs to write the vegetable that Oliver finds on each day of the week, and what he eats (for example, rhubarb pie).

- Discuss the different vegetables that Oliver has eaten. Ask the children to remember with their partner – finding the answer in the book if needed – which part of each vegetable we eat. Establish that potatoes grow under the ground. Explain that they need to be dug up rather than pulled up. Ask children which of these vegetables they have eaten and which they would like to try. If possible, provide some of the vegetables that can be eaten raw or cold (such as carrots, cabbage, beetroot or peas) and some pea pods to shell. You could then encourage the children to improve on Oliver's descriptions (good; very good) with their own positive or negative comments.

- Ask: *What do you think Oliver has learned over this week?* Encourage the children to talk widely about Oliver, how he felt at the beginning of the story and how he possibly felt at the end. Ask: *What* stopped Oliver from eating vegetables earlier? Do you think finding the vegetables helped Oliver to eat them? If so, why? Remind the children about other things that they know about Oliver, encouraging them to provide evidence from the text. For example: he likes to be active and outside – we know this because he wants to walk, he rushes outside after the rain, he plays football; he is not a nervous person – he is relaxed about animals, he is not nervous about trying the vegetables. Agree therefore that we can infer that it is something about finding the vegetables growing in the ground, or his bargain with Grandpa or the excitement of being somewhere new that made him happy to eat the vegetables.

- Introduce the term 'theme' to the group. Explain that a theme is a main idea in a story. Ask: What might the theme be in Oliver's Vegetables? Discuss the children's ideas, encouraging them to elaborate on their thoughts and to listen to each other (for example, 'vegetables are great' or 'be brave and try something new' or 'new places give us new courage' or 'healthy living').

Ask the children, whenever appropriate, to revisit the text to exemplify/support the answers.

Encourage the children to read aloud back to the group when referring back to the text – praise clear, confident and expressive reading.

ASSESSMENT OPPORTUNITIES

The following bank of question prompts provides a quick and easy means of monitoring the children's comprehension skills and understanding of the text. The children's answers to a question must be supported by evidence from the text.

Understanding
- Name three vegetables that Oliver tries in the book.
- On what day does he find peas?
- What vegetable in Grandpa's garden do slugs and snails like?
- How long does Oliver stay with his grandparents?

Inferences
- Why do you think that Oliver has not eaten his vegetables before?
- Why do you think Oliver changed his mind about the vegetables?
- What sort of things does Oliver like to do?
- What might Oliver's mother say when she finds out why everyone is laughing at the end?

Predicting
- Do you think Oliver will eat his vegetables in future?

Language, structure and presentation
- How is the story organised?
- Separate these words into root word + ending:
  - proudly
  - wonderful
  - nearest
  - rushed
- What word is used in the story to describe the deal that Oliver strikes with his Grandpa?

Themes and conventions
- What is the main lesson we might learn from Oliver's Vegetables?

▼ SESSION 1: BEWARE OF THE DOG

SESSION AIMS

Focusing on the main character through the opening events.

READ

- Look at the cover together. Ask the children if they know *The Gruffalo*. Tell them that *Stick Man* is written by the same author and illustrator team, and that Stick Man first appeared in the story *The Gruffalo's Child*.

- Read *Stick Man* aloud, encouraging the children to join in with the repeated phrases. As you read, pause at various points, for example, when the dog chases Stick Man, when Stick Man is free from the nest and when Stick Man is lying on the grate, to ask the children to predict what is going to happen next.

- Return to the beginning of the story and ask volunteers to read the first four spreads (up to '"…weave into my nest."') Check the children's understanding of the events:
  - Where does Stick Man live?
  - Who does he live with?
  - Why does he leave the family tree?
  - What is the first disaster to happen to Stick Man?
  - What does Stick Man say when he is stolen?
  - Why does the girl throw Stick Man in the river?
  - How does he end up in a nest?

- Ask: *What are the two main things that happen at the beginning of this story?* (Stick Man is taken first by a dog and then by a girl for Pooh-sticks.) Ensure that the children are familiar with the game of Pooh-sticks. If not, explain that two or more people each find a stick; then, standing on a bridge over a flowing river – looking upstream – they all throw their stick in the water at the same time. The players rush to the other side of the bridge and the person whose stick appears first from under the bridge is the winner.

During reading

- Move around the group and 'tune in' to hear individuals read aloud. Encourage and praise good expression.

REVISIT AND RESPOND

Bring the group back together and discuss some of the points below to help the children think about the first four spreads in more depth.

Note: Since there are only 20 minutes for each session, you are advised to focus on only one or two of the elements that are listed below.

- Return to the beginning of the book. Look together at the title page and then at the first page of the story. Ask the children to think about Stick Man. What does he look like? What sort of character might he be? Do they think that Stick Man looks like a stick? Could he do something to make himself look more like a person? Ask: *What is the most important thing in the world to Stick Man? Does he have a happy life? Why does he say "I'M STICK MAN, that's me!"* (He's telling everyone that he's not a stick, he's a person.)

- Consider how Stick Man might be feeling on the different spreads. Look at the expression on his face in the different pictures. What do the children think he's feeling when he's at home with his family/being chased by the dog/being thrown into the water/being made into a nest?

- Ask: *What starts the story off?* Agree that it is being taken by the dog while out for a run. Discuss which is worse for Stick Man: being played with by a dog or being thrown into a river. Help the children articulate any thoughts on the dog's teeth and saliva and the horror of being thrown and fetched before helping them to see that, actually, it is being thrown into the river and drifting so far from home that sets his story in motion. Discuss how the story might have ended if the girl hadn't picked up Stick Man for Pooh-sticks. Perhaps he would have walked – rather bruised and messy – back to his tree and never left again. Ask: *Is the dog wrong to play with Stick Man? Is the girl naughty to throw Stick Man into the river?*

- Discuss where the children think this part of the book is set. (in a town park) Look together at the illustrations and challenge each child to come up with a different disaster for Stick Man (for example, he might be put in the bin, picked up by a crow, run over by the girl on roller skates, given to the child in the pushchair, used as a bookmark, and so on).

- Ask the children to tell you what is special about the language of the story. Agree that it rhymes and has a strong beat – like a poem. Challenge each child, or pair of children, to find two words in this section that rhyme (for example: tree/three, jog/dog, stick/trick, and so on). Tell the rest of the group to say whether the two rhyming words spell their shared vowel sound the same (stick/trick) or differently (throw/go, on/swan).

Ask the children, whenever appropriate, to revisit the text to exemplify/support the answers.

Encourage the children to read aloud back to the group when referring back to the text – praise clear, confident and expressive reading.

ASSESSMENT OPPORTUNITIES

The following bank of question prompts provides a quick and easy means of monitoring the children's comprehension skills and understanding of the text. The children's answers to a question must be supported by evidence from the text.

Understanding
- Why does Stick Man leave the house at the beginning of the story?
- Why does the dog catch Stick Man?
- Why do the dog and the boy stop playing with Stick Man?
- What does Stick Man say when he is being thrown to the dog?
- Where is Stick Man when the swan finds him?

Inferences
- What does Stick Man feel when the dog is put on a lead?
- What does the frog think when he sees Stick Man in the water?

- Why is the swan building a nest?
- What does the boy think of his dog?

Predicting
- What do you think is going to happen to Stick Man?

Main ideas
- What is the main problem that Stick Man has?

Language, structure and presentation
- How does the story start?
- What repeated phrase does Stick Man say when he is mistaken for a stick?

▼ SESSION 2: CHANGING SEASONS

SESSION AIMS

Tracking the journey through the seasons; looking at the author's use of repetitive language.

READ

- Re-read the beginning of *Stick Man* and continue up to spread 8, where Stick Man is sitting sadly in the puddle saying, '"Will I ever get back to the family tree?"'. Ask the children to work in pairs to count all the different uses people have made of Stick Man. Tell them to discuss with a partner which use they like best and which use they think is worst for poor old Stick Man. Spend a moment empathising with Stick Man's dreadful plight:
  - What do you think Stick Man's family think has happened to him?
  - How does Stick Man feel as he's sitting in the cold puddle?
- Clarify the meaning of 'deserted', 'drifts' and 'boomerang', encouraging the children to attempt a definition in each case before telling them the meaning.

During reading

- Move around the group and 'tune in' to hear individuals read aloud. Encourage and praise good expression.

REVISIT AND RESPOND

Bring the group back together and discuss some of the points below, focusing on spreads 5 to 8.

Note: Since there are only 20 minutes for each session, you are advised to focus on only one or two of the elements that are listed below.

- Consider how the changing seasons are depicted through the book. Return to the first spread and ask the children: *What time of year was it when Stick Man went for his jog?* Help them to see that although there are leaves on the trees, they are small and this shows that it is spring. Explain that bluebells and cherry blossom are spring flowers. If you have time and resources, challenge the children to find out when swans lay their eggs (April to May)

and how long it takes for the eggs to hatch (about five weeks). Point out the following animals on spread 4: swan, frog, heron, great crested grebe, moorhen and female mallard duck.

- Spend a few moments practising the months of the year and talking about which months fall in which season. Ask: *When do you think Stick Man is used for the sandcastle?* (probably during the school holidays in July or August) Look at spread 7 and ask the pairs to discuss in which season each event takes place. Help them to see the clues to the changing season: trees in full leaf in the summer, roses in bloom in the summer, apples on the tree at the end of the summer, leaves starting to turn at the beginning of autumn, leaves brown in the middle of autumn and snow at the beginning of winter. Look at spread 8 for clues here about the time of year: it has snowed, it's dark (look at the street lights) but it's still early enough to be outside playing.
- Help the children to see that the story is organised around the seasons and that this gives it a shape or 'structure'. Talk about how by seeing the different seasons passing, we understand that Stick Man has been away from his family for a very long time.
- Allow time for the children to enjoy the illustrations on each spread in turn, sharing different details of activities or plants or animals with a partner and then sharing them with the group.
- Talk about the author's use of repetitive language. Ask: *What does Stick Man say each time he is picked up?* Ask the children to find the different instances of this chorus up to spread 8 and to tell you what is the same (the structure of the first and last lines; all of the middle) and what is different (some of the words for the first and last lines). Ask: *Why are some of the words written in italics and why are some written in capitals?* (to give emphasis) Ask children to make up what Stick Man might say at the different points on spread 7 (for example, 'I'm not a hook! Can't she see/I'm Stick Man, I'm Stick Man, I'M STICK MAN, that's me!'). What other repetitive lines has the author used? Ask the children to work in pairs to find repetition and then share their ideas.

- Look at the themes of identity and home. Ask the children: *What is Stick Man's main problem?* (that he looks like a stick) Ask: *What does he want more than anything else?* (to go home) Ask the children to search through the first eight spreads to find places where these two themes crop up.

Ask the children, whenever appropriate, to revisit the text to exemplify/support the answers.

Encourage the children to read aloud back to the group when referring back to the text – praise clear, confident and expressive reading.

ASSESSMENT OPPORTUNITIES

The following bank of question prompts provides a quick and easy means of monitoring the children's comprehension skills and understanding of the text. The children's answers to a question must be supported by evidence from the text.

Understanding
- How does Stick Man get free of the nest?
- What happens to Stick Man at the seaside?
- Name three other uses people have for Stick Man.
- What happens to Stick Man in the snow?
- What happens to the snowman that the boy makes?

Inferences
- How long has Stick Man been away from the family tree?
- Do you think that the children are naughty to use Stick Man?
- How does Stick Man feel when he is free of the nest?
- How does Stick Man feel when he's free of the sandcastle?
- How does Stick Man get free of the snowman?

Language, structure and presentation
- What does Stick Man say when he has been mistaken for a stick?
- What does the narrator (the storyteller) say when the dad with a spade comes towards him?

- What does the word 'weave' tell you that the swan is going to do with Stick Man? Is it a better word than 'put'?
- How do you know that Stick Man has been away from home a long time?

Predicting
- Do you think Stick Man will ever get home?

Themes and conventions
- What is Stick Man's main problem?
- Where is Stick Man's favourite place in the world?

SESSION AIMS

Focusing on the climax of the book – from Stick Man at his lowest point to his meeting with Santa.

READ

- Ask the children to recap on the story so far before reading it aloud from the beginning again. Encourage the children to join in where they can, in particular for the lines that repeat.
- Look together at spread 9. Ask:
  - What time of year is it here? How do we know?
  - Why are people singing outside the church?
  - Who has spotted Stick Man in this scene?
  - What animals can you spot in the picture?
- Explore the next two spreads:
  - Why have the singers collected wood?
  - What's going to happen to Stick Man? (Help any children unfamiliar with open fires to understand that the fire will be lit in the house.)
  - What does Stick Man hear as he lies on the grate?
  - What clues can you find that it is Santa up the chimney?
  - Who is the 'Stuck Man'?
- Look together at spread 12, where Santa lands with a bump. Ask: *Why are the words written so large?* (because the situation is so wonderful and so surprising) Challenge the children to find the following in the picture: Christmas cards, Christmas tree, candles, presents, Christmas decorations, the Gruffalo! Can they also find out what the time is when Santa arrives? Encourage the children to talk about their own Christmas traditions.

During reading

- Move around the group and 'tune in' to hear individuals read aloud. Encourage and praise good expression.

REVISIT AND RESPOND

Bring the group back together and discuss some of the points below.

Note: Since there are only 20 minutes for each session, you are advised to focus on only one or two of the elements that are listed below.

- Look at the image of Stick Man lying in the grate. Ask: *How does Stick Man feel now?* (very tired and sad; he has lost all hope) Ask the children to pretend for a minute that they don't know that Stick Man is going to be saved. Tell them to discuss with a partner what could happen next and how Stick Man could escape. Talk about the story so far. Point out that, from the moment Stick Man was picked up by the dog, things have got worse and worse for him: he's been taken further and further from home until he has finally given up hope.
- Talk about the children's ideas for different endings. As the story so far has had a simple structure involving lots of different things happening to Stick Man, perhaps the rest of the story could be about more things happening to him until it is spring again. For example, a dog could take Stick Man out of the fire, a bird could fly him nearer home, a hiker stick him in her backpack, a child take him for a toy, each one travelling nearer and nearer to the family tree.
- Consider how Stick Man is rescued by Santa in the nick of time. Discuss other stories that the children know where the main character is saved from almost certain disaster by some sudden luck (for example, *Toy Story 3* when the main characters are saved from the furnace by the aliens working the claw). Ask: *Can you think of a story where the main character was not saved? Or did not have a happy ending?* Agree that it is usual in adventure stories for everything to end well for the main character, though after some disasters.
- Point out the reversals (or opposites) on spread 12: Stick Man helps someone rather than being used; Santa knows who Stick Man is and doesn't think he is a stick; everything is happy rather than sad.

Returning to the first point here, draw the children's attention to the fact that all through the story, Stick Man is unable to help himself but the first time he can help someone else, he does – and this saves him! Remind the children that mistaken identity is a theme of the story. Tell them that this theme ends happily here.

- Remind the children that, like many poems, *Stick Man* rhymes and has a strong rhythm. Tell them to clap along with the rhythm as you read the words on spread 9. Ask: *Which words rhyme here? Are the endings spelled the same or differently? Can you find any words on the same line that start with the same sound? Can you find any repeated cluster of words?* Talk about how these elements are often found in poems and give an extra sadness to this passage.

- Turn to the end of spread 11 and ask the children: *Can you find any rhyming words that are on the same line? Can you find words that start with the same sound on the same line? Can you find some pairs of verbs (doing words)?* Talk about how these elements seem to make the passage sound happier – something is about to happen.

Ask the children, whenever appropriate, to revisit the text to exemplify/support the answers.

Encourage the children to read aloud back to the group when referring back to the text – praise clear, confident and expressive reading.

ASSESSMENT OPPORTUNITIES

The following bank of question prompts provides a quick and easy means of monitoring the children's comprehension skills and understanding of the text. The children's answers to a question must be supported by evidence from the text.

Understanding
- Why does the girl pick up Stick Man?
- What does Stick Man think about on the grate?
- What does Stick Man hear up the chimney?

Inferences
- How does Stick Man feel as he lies in the grate?
- How does Stick Man feel when he sees Santa?
- Why does Santa know Stick Man's name?

Predicting
- Do you think that Santa can help Stick Man get home?

Main ideas
- What is the main event in this part of the story?

Language, structure and presentation
- Why is a grate a bad place for Stick Man to sleep?
- What is another way of saying 'Stick Man is weary'?
- Why are the words 'And Santa falls into the room with a thump!' larger than the other words in the rest of the book?

Themes and conventions
- Did you expect Stick Man to be rescued from the grate?
- Does Santa think that Stick Man is a stick?

▼ SESSION 4: HOME AT LAST

SESSION AIMS

Remembering the story as a whole and learning to tell own version, using some of the same language.

READ

- Start reading from spread 12 and ask the children to remember how Stick Man has saved Santa. Read on to the end of the book together. Pause to look at the sad image of Stick Man's children lying in the bed. Ask: *It's Christmas Eve – why are the children sad?* Agree that it is because their father is missing. Talk about traditions such as hanging up stockings on Christmas Eve.

- Imagine how the children and their mother feel when Stick Man returns. Remind the children that 'getting home' is one of the themes of the story.

- Look at Stick Man's house on this page and the previous one, thinking about the following:

  - What toys do the children have? What are they made of?

  - What are the plates made of?

  - What are the chairs made of?

  - Who else lives in the house with Stick Man and his family?

- Point out the holly and mistletoe and explain that these are plants associated with Christmas. Explain that mistletoe is sometimes hung up in houses at this time of year and people kiss underneath it.

During reading

- Move around the group and 'tune in' to hear individuals read aloud. Encourage and praise good expression.

REVISIT AND RESPOND

Bring the group back together and discuss some of the points below on the structure and the language of *Stick Man*.

Note: Since there are only 20 minutes for each session, you are advised to focus on only one or two of the elements that are listed below.

- Take a large piece of paper and with the group map out Stick Man's journey. Encourage the children to look through the book to find the different locations, and to decide where they should go on the map. When you've mapped out the park, the river, the seaside, the second town and the second park, let the children take turns to add Stick Man having his different disasters in the different locations.

- Provide the children with figures to represent the key characters: Stick Man, Stick Man's family, the dog, the girl, the swan, the family at the seaside, a boy, another girl, Santa. Ask the children in pairs, or as a group, to sequence the characters and use them to remember the story. (If necessary, explain that you haven't provided all the characters and that these are enough to tell the main events of the story.) Ask: *Does it matter in which order the events come?* As a group, experiment with the order of events. Agree that the girl who plays Pooh-sticks needs to come before the swan and the sandcastle, but that the events in the middle could come before or after these, and could come in any order. (The boy who makes a snowman and the girl collecting wood on Christmas Eve must go at the end.) Explain that the river needs to come before the seaside because rivers flow to the sea.

- Ask the children to work in pairs to retell the story to each other using the characters. Then encourage them to use ideas from the book or their own ideas to tell their version of *Stick Man*.

- Ask: *What is special about the way* Stick Man *is written?* Agree that it rhymes and has a regular beat, like a poem. Read the opening and ask the children to clap the beat as you read. Create a rhyme challenge for the children. Give them a series of vowel sounds and see which child, or pair, can be the first to find a rhyming pair of words with that vowel sound. Ask: *Apart from rhyme and rhythm, what other poetry techniques are there in the story?* Agree there are a number of repeated lines. (Beware…, I'm not a…, and the chorus.)

• Ask the children to think about the story as a whole. Tell them to share their favourite parts with a partner, and then with the rest of the group. Ask questions, encouraging the children to make inferences based on the text: *How do you think Stick Man might feel after his adventure? What do you think he will say to his family? How can Stick Man stop himself being taken by someone next time he goes out?* (Perhaps he could put on some clothes. Perhaps he could get a whistle to blow when he is in trouble.) Ask: *Will he have any happy memories?* (Perhaps he might decide to take his children to the seaside, or to wait up and see Santa the following year.)

Ask the children, whenever appropriate, to revisit the text to exemplify/support the answers.

Encourage the children to read aloud back to the group when referring back to the text – praise clear, confident and expressive reading.

ASSESSMENT OPPORTUNITIES

The following bank of question prompts provides a quick and easy means of monitoring the children's comprehension skills and understanding of the text. The children's answers to a question must be supported by evidence from the text.

Understanding
• Who does Stick Man live with?
• How does he get into the river?
• Name three things that Stick Man is used for.
• How does Stick Man finally get home?
• Do you think the animals and people were mean to Stick Man?

Inferences
• For how long is Stick Man away from home?
• Why does he fall asleep in the grate rather than escaping?

• How does Stick Man feel as he sits in the snowy puddle?
• Why does Stick Man keep saying, '"I'm Stick Man!"'?

Predicting
• Do you think that Stick Man will ever leave the house again?

Main ideas
• Write down the four main events of the book.

Language, structure and presentation
• What does Stick Man say when he is mistaken for a stick?
• How is the story organised?

Themes and conventions
• Did you expect Stick Man to make it home?
• What should Stick Man do next time he wants to go for a run?

▼ SESSION 1: OUT IN SPACE

SESSION AIMS

Identifying the characters and setting; predicting what might happen.

READ

- Ask the children to read the first three spreads independently. Invite them to consider some of these questions:
  - Do you think there is one main character in this story or several? What makes you think this?
  - Where do you think the aliens live?
  - How do the aliens travel?
  - What do these aliens really love?
  - What do you think might happen next?

During reading

- Listen as the children are reading, and praise individuals for clarity and good expression.

REVISIT AND RESPOND

Bring the group back together and discuss some of the points below, which relate to the covers, inner pages and first three spreads.

Note: Since there are only 20 minutes for each session, you are advised to focus on only one or two of the elements that are listed below.

- Explore the cover illustrations. Read the title and the text on the back together. Ask: *Who is this book about?* Explain the word *zany* and ask: *What do you think the words 'zany' and 'hilarious' in the blurb sentence tell us about the style in which this story is written? What does the author mean by 'laugh your pants off!'? Why has she said this instead of the usual saying, 'Laugh your socks off!'?* Talk about other funny stories the children have enjoyed and what they liked about them.

- Discuss what type of story has alien characters and what usually happens. Invite children to recall any stories they have read featuring aliens. Encourage prediction about the style and content of this book based on their prior knowledge.

- Turn to the decorative inner page and discuss the different underpants. Ask: *Which underpants do you like best and why? Can you describe your favourite pattern? Who might like the underpants with the skull and crossbones? How do you know this? Can you describe the underpants the aliens might like the most?*

- Explore the illustration showing where the aliens live and discuss what you see together. Ask: *How does this planet differ from Earth? How can you tell the planet is in space? Why do you think the aliens have decorated their planet with sculptures of underpants? Have you seen the same strange symbols that the aliens have on their sculptures anywhere in your own home?* (washing symbols on clothes) *What do you think they mean? What are the aliens reading? What sort of information do you think they are looking for? Describe the alien families. Do they have any children or pets? How do you know?*

- Re-read the text on the first spread together and make comparisons with poetry (for example, regular pattern, rhyming couplets, starting sentences with 'So', 'But'). Identify the rhyming words at the end of alternate lines. Continue this comparison when exploring the second and third spreads.

- Draw attention to the two ellipses and discuss why the author has used them. Pause after reading 'big surprise…', and 'YOU…' to ask what children think happens next. As you read the second spread together, remember to emphasise the word in capitals, 'YOU', and the final sentence ending with an exclamation mark. After reading, ask: *Where are the aliens going and why? What do their spaceship stickers tell us about what they think of underpants? Which sticker do you like best and why? What sort of 'underpants' sticker would you design?*

- Read the third spread together and discuss the meaning of *radar*. Ask: *Who uses radar? What is it for? What will the aliens do when it blinks and bleeps? What do you think happens next?*

Ask the children, whenever appropriate, to revisit the text to exemplify/support the answers.

Encourage the children to read aloud back to the group when referring back to the text – praise clear, confident and expressive reading.

ASSESSMENT OPPORTUNITIES

The following bank of question prompts provides a quick and easy means of monitoring the children's comprehension skills and understanding of the text. The children's answers to a question must be supported by evidence from the text.

Understanding
- What did you find out about the aliens from this section?
- Can you describe the alien spaceships?
- What did you discover about the inside of the spaceships?
- What do you recognise on the illustration of Earth?

Inferences
- Why do you think the aliens are travelling to Earth?
- What do you think aliens like reading about?
- Why do you think there are no underpants in space?
- How can you tell that aliens love underpants of every shape and size?

Predicting
- How do you think the aliens felt when they spotted a washing line of underpants on the radar?
- What part do you think the spaceships play in the story? Do you think the aliens could collect underpants without them?
- What do you think will happen next, now the aliens have spotted some underpants?

Main ideas
- What is the main event in this section?

Language, structure and presentation
- What do you notice about the title and the first sentence? Can you think of another sentence the author could have used to start the story?
- How do you know that this story is written like a poem? Can you describe the patterns in the way the words are organised? (Try substituting the second rhyming word in each couplet for a non-rhyming word, for example, surprise/shock, knew/thought, breeze/wind. Read the whole section with the substitutes and discuss the difference this makes to the flow of the text.)
- Identify the connecting words, 'But', 'So', between the lines in the first spread. Read this page with and without these words and talk about how the flow is disrupted. Which do the children prefer?

Themes and conventions
- Is this a fiction or non-fiction book? How do you know?
- What clues can you find about the type of story this is from exploring the cover and reading this section? (fantasy tale/funny tale)

▼ SESSION 2: DOWN TO EARTH

SESSION AIMS

Considering and evaluating different viewpoints, attending to and building on the contributions of others.

READ

Ask the children to read spreads 4 to 6 independently, thinking about some of the following questions:

- Where have the aliens landed?
- Why are the aliens dancing with delight when they arrive?
- How can you tell that humans live here?
- What did the aliens use to record their visit?
- What did the aliens play with and what games did they play?
- What do you think the cat thinks of these strange visitors?

During reading

- Listen to individual children read, praising good clear expression. Encourage them to attempt unfamiliar or difficult words to help their understanding.

REVISIT AND RESPOND

Bring the group back together and discuss some of the points below.

Note: Since there are only 20 minutes for each session, you are advised to focus on only one or two of the elements that are listed below.

- Recall the comparisons with poetry made after reading the first section and ask children for evidence that this section is written in the same way. The orange underpants are described as 'like satsumas'. Why do the children think the author has used this word to describe the colour? Ask: *Which word does 'satsuma' rhyme with? Would the text's sound and meaning be as effective if the author had used the word 'tangerine' instead?*

- Explain that the words 'bloomers' and 'longjohns' are old-fashioned words for underpants and make links between the people they belong to (Granny, Grandpa). Ask: *Which words describe Mum's pants?* ('pink frilly knickers') Can the children find them on the washing line?

- Ask the children to find the speech marks indicating the two words that the aliens chant at the start of this section. What other punctuation do children notice? Discuss how these words should be read, given that one is an expressive sound and the other is in capital letters with an exclamation mark. Remind the children that this is a funny story, and so perhaps their interpretations should be amusing. Talk about what an alien voice might be like. Perhaps children recall voices they have heard in cartoons or films. Ask: *How do you think the aliens' voices in this story will sound – high and squeaky, loud and booming or quiet and hissy?* Invite children to dance around in the role of aliens, taking turns to chant the words using their own ideas of an alien voice. Praise individuals for imaginative and funny interpretations. Encourage children to comment on the interpretations of their peers and build upon them positively with new versions.

- Look at the illustration of the spaceship. Ask: *What shape is it? It has a rounded base so how does it keep level on the ground? Where is the door? Can you see any windows?* Explain that spaceships that are flat and round are sometimes called 'flying saucers'. *Why is this?* Recall the images from the second spread and discuss whether these spaceships look like saucers.

- Find the illustration of the alien dancing in Granny's bloomers while others record these antics. Ask: *Why do you think the aliens want to record their visit? Who will they show the recording to when they return home? Do you take photographs and films on holiday? Have you ever taken any funny recordings? Which special events did you record?*

- Talk about the games the aliens are playing with the underpants. Discuss why they choose Grandpa's longjohns to make the slide, rather than the red or pink ones on either side. Ask: *How is the slide described? What does this word tells us about the sort of ride we would have on it? Have you ever made a slide out of something unusual? When the aliens played hide and seek, Mum's knickers made a funny place to hide. Can you describe a funny place to hide?*

- After reading spreads 4 to 6, ask the children what they think the aliens are going to do next. Prompt with questions such as: *Will they take anything with them? Will someone catch them? What will the cat do?* Discuss the various responses together and make positive evaluations of them, leading to new ideas where possible.

Ask the children, whenever appropriate, to revisit the text to exemplify/support the answers.

Encourage the children to read aloud back to the group when referring back to the text – praise clear, confident and expressive reading.

ASSESSMENT OPPORTUNITIES

The following bank of question prompts provides a quick and easy means of monitoring the children's comprehension skills and understanding of the text. The children's answers to a question must be supported by evidence from the text.

Understanding
- How has the setting changed from the first section? What is different about it?
- Where did the aliens land their spaceship?
- What did the aliens get up to when they landed?
- What do you think the aliens discovered about where humans live?

Inferences
- What do you know about the people who live in the house? Do they have any pets?
- Which underpants did the aliens like the sight of best of all?

- Why do you think the underpants on the washing line are different sizes and shapes? What does this tell you about the people who live there?

Predicting
- What do you think the aliens will think of the cat? Will they be frightened or keen to play?
- How do you think the aliens felt when they arrived in the garden? What would they do first?
- Do you think the aliens asked the family for permission before they landed in their garden? Which words tell us they did not?
- What do you think the aliens will do after they finish playing games?

Language, structure and presentation
- Which rhyming words do you like best in this section?
- Can you think of words to finish these descriptions of underpants: orange like…; green like…; red like…; spotted like a…?

Themes and conventions
- What do you think is the funniest illustration in this section? How does the illustrator make the aliens appear funny?
- Which character has the funniest actions? Why do you think this?
- What would you do if you found an alien in your garden?

▼ SESSION 3: DARING COMPETITIONS, SILLY GAMES!

SESSION AIMS

Making inferences on the basis of what is said and done.

READ

- Ask the children to read spreads 7 to 9, bearing in mind the following questions:
  - Can you describe the daring competition the aliens held using the longjohns?
  - Can you describe the 'Upside-Down-Pant Races'?
  - How did the aliens make use of the 'pingy pants elastic'?
  - What did they fly from their spaceships in the silly games?

During reading

- Move around the group listening in as children read. Remind them to check that they understand the text, particularly as they tackle unfamiliar or difficult words.

REVISIT AND RESPOND

Bring the group back together and discuss some of the points below.

Note: Since there are only 20 minutes for each session, you are advised to focus on only one or two of the elements that are listed below.

- Look at the illustration on the spread 7. Talk about the meaning of 'daring'. Ask: *What is daring about squeezing lots of aliens into the longjohns? Which words give us the answer?* (just one peg) Encourage children to explain what would happen if the peg came off the washing line. Ask: *Why did the aliens choose the longjohns? Could they hold the competition with the heart pants instead? Why not?* Compare this to silly competitions humans hold and the records they try to break, such as how many people can fit into a small car at the same time.

- Explore the silly 'Upside-Down-Pant Races' on the next spread. Ask: *Why does the race have this name? Why is it described as silly? Which alien do you think is wearing the pants in the funniest place? Why is it silly to run with something over your head?* Discuss whether the children have ever taken part in any sort of silly races themselves – for example, a dressing-up race or three-legged race. Ask: *How do these races work? Can you make up silly names for them? Which do you think is funniest – human races or alien races? Why do you think this?*

- Explore the illustration on spread 9 and re-read the text. Ask: *What are the aliens doing? Why do you think the text and illustration have been presented in this way? What is different about this page? What do you think the illustrator wanted to show?* (how high the aliens were bouncing) *What equipment do humans use to help them to bounce in the air like this?* (trampolines) *Why do you think the aliens are using underpants with 'pingy' elastic? What does the word 'pingy' mean? Can you make the sound it describes? Do you think 'pants-tastic' is a good word to describe the fun the aliens are having? Which word has the author changed to create this new nonsense word?* (fantastic) *Do you think it works well on this page?* Challenge the children to make up another nonsense word ending in 'tastic' to describe the alien races and competitions (for example, 'peg-tastic' or 'silly-tastic').

- Find the image of underpants flying from a spaceship and ask: *Do you think the aliens like flying their underpants through the air? Could you have a silly human race by running along flying lines of pants in the air behind you?*

Ask the children, whenever appropriate, to revisit the text to exemplify/support the answers.

Encourage the children to read aloud back to the group when referring to the text – praise clear, confident and expressive reading.

ASSESSMENT OPPORTUNITIES

The following bank of question prompts provides a quick and easy means of monitoring the children's comprehension skills and understanding of the text. The children's answers to a question must be supported by evidence from the text.

Understanding

- What happens in this section of the story?
- How do the aliens amuse themselves?
- What do they use as props in their games and competitions?
- Describe how to take part in an 'Upside-Down-Pants Race' in your own words.

Inferences

- Can you find the alien that seems to be using a tape recorder or mobile phone? Both of these gadgets will only record or transmit sound; what sounds do you think the aliens are making as they take part in this daring competition?
- What word makes you think that the aliens are having great fun? (pants-tastic)
- Do you think the aliens know about humans? Why do you think this?
- Do you think the aliens would be frightened if a human appeared?
- How do you think the aliens and the humans who live in the house would get along?

Predicting

- How many aliens do you think will fit inside the longjohns? What does it depend on?
- How could the daring longjohn competition go wrong? What could happen to the aliens if this happened?
- What could happen to the aliens who are racing with the underpants over their heads?
- Where did they hold their games? Why do you think no one has discovered them yet? Where are the humans?
- What do you think will happen next? What will the aliens will do when they get too tired for races?

Language, structure and presentation

- Why does the author use exclamation marks after the words 'Upside-Down-Pant Races' and 'pingy pants elastic'? Do you think this punctuation emphasises how funny the words are?
- Do you think 'zinging' is a good word to describe the movement of the aliens as they bounce through the air? Can you think of alternative words?
- How would you explain the meaning of 'competition' to a younger child?
- Which rhyming words in this section are the most/ least interesting?
- What do you notice about the ninth spread? Why do you think you have to turn the page round to read the text and explore the long illustration?

Themes and conventions

- If you held a 'funniest category' competition, what do you think the funniest event/word/alien/ illustration from this section would be?
- If you were writing a funny story about these aliens, what sort of competitions and races involving underpants would you invent?

SESSION 4: OFF IN A HURRY!

SESSION AIMS

Explaining and discussing their understanding of
books they have read for themselves.

READ

- Ask the children to read the final three spreads (10
  to 12) independently. Invite them to consider some
  of these questions:
  - Who stole the underpants off the line? How do
    you know?
  - What happens that causes the aliens to fly away
    in a hurry?
  - Which two human characters do we meet for
    the first time in this section?
  - Who are the two animals appearing in this
    section?
  - Do you think this is a good way to end the story?
    Why do you think this? Were you surprised by
    this ending?

During reading

- As you listen to children's reading and discussion,
  praise confident attempts to tackle difficult
  or unfamiliar words, and comment positively
  on clear explanations that demonstrate good
  understanding.

REVISIT AND RESPOND

Bring the group back together and discuss some of
the points below.

Note: Since there are only 20 minutes for each
session, you are advised to focus on only one or two
of the elements that are listed below.

- Read the tenth spread again. Ask: *What is meant
  by the first sentence? What was it that the
  neighbour's naughty dog did not do? What could
  next-door's funny game be if it is about underpants
  going missing? Who really took the underpants
  from the line? How can you tell from the illustration
  alone? Which sentence names the culprits?*

- Discuss the actions of the aliens. Ask the children
  if they think the aliens should take the underpants
  without asking. Can they say what word we use for
  this action? (stealing) Ask: *Is it right to steal another
  person's possessions? Have you ever taken anything
  that did not belong to you? How did you feel? Has
  anyone ever taken something of yours? How did
  you feel? Do you think the aliens should have asked
  permission to take the underpants? How could they
  have done this?*

- Explore the different punctuation in this section.
  Talk about why the word 'ALIENS' is in capital
  letters. Find the exclamation marks and read the
  preceding words or sentences with emphasis.
  Discuss the need for the ellipsis after the word
  'fast'. Ask: *What did you expect to happen after
  this pause? Were you surprised by the different
  scene that followed when you turned over
  the page?*

- Talk about the author's use of poetic convention.
  What do the children notice about the first word
  of every line in this section? Briefly look back
  through the book to check whether the same thing
  happens throughout. Ask: *Do you usually put a
  capital letter at the start of every line in your own
  writing?* Discuss how the lines of poems often start
  with capital letters and suggest that this is strong
  evidence – along with the rhyming words and
  shape of the text – that the story is written like
  a poem.

- Talk about significant events in this final section of
  the story. Ask: *Why did the aliens zoom off? What
  does the author mean when she says the aliens
  are used to leaving fast? Do you think this has
  happened before? When they left in a hurry did
  they leave any aliens behind? How do you know
  this? Describe this alien. Why is the cat stalking up
  to the washing basket? Why is the cat winking at
  the reader?*

- Consider how the ending might have changed
  if Mum or the boy had spotted the aliens. Ask
  children for ideas on a possible sequel to the story.

Ask the children, whenever appropriate, to revisit the text to exemplify/support the answers.

Encourage the children to read aloud back to the group when referring to the text – praise clear, confident and expressive reading.

ASSESSMENT OPPORTUNITIES

The following bank of question prompts provides a quick and easy means of monitoring the children's comprehension skills and understanding of the text. The children's answers to a question must be supported by evidence from the text.

Understanding
- Where does the dog live? How do you know this?
- What evidence is there on spread 11 that the aliens left in spaceships?
- Can you explain why the boy is checking inside his underpants?
- Which of these characters know that the aliens came to visit – Mum, the boy, the cat or the dog?

Inferences
- Why do you think Mum is looking worried as she looks over the sheet on the washing line?
- If you were going to interview Mum after the underpants went missing, what questions would you ask her?
- Why do you think one alien was left behind? Where do you think it was when the others left in a hurry?
- Do you think the boy likes aliens? What items in his bedroom make you think this?
- What questions would you ask the aliens about their visit to Earth?

Predicting
- What do you think will happen to the alien that was left behind? Will the others come back for him/her?
- What do you think the boy would do if there was an alien lurking in his underpants?
- Do you think the aliens will come back to the same garden for more underpants? What makes you think this?

Language, structure and presentation
- What words describe the sound and movement of the spaceships leaving? What does this tell you about the way the aliens left?
- What is a neighbour?
- What does it mean if you are to blame for something?
- What do you think the author meant by 'lurks inside, unseen'? Can you think of different words to say the same thing?
- What question would you most like to ask your favourite alien?

Themes and conventions
- This story has humour, rhyme and fantasy. Can you give an example of each theme from this section?
- The story events take place in three different settings (alien planet, spaceship, Earth): can you describe each one?
- Would you like to meet the aliens? What would you give them as a welcome gift?

▼ SESSION 1: INTRODUCING THE WITCH

Identifying the characters and setting; predicting what might happen.

READ

- Ask the children to read the first two spreads independently, bearing in mind the following questions:
  - Who do you think is the main character in the story?
  - Where do you think she is flying to?
  - Who is flying with her?
  - What do you think might happen next?

During reading

- Move among the group and focus attention on individual readers, giving praise for clear expressive reading. Encourage children to check that the text makes sense to them as they read.

REVISIT AND RESPOND

Bring the group back together and discuss some of the points below, which focus on the covers, inner pages and first two spreads.

Note: Since there are only 20 minutes for each session, you are advised to focus on only one or two of the elements that are listed below.

- Explore the illustration on the front and back covers together. What do the children think they tell us about what the book is about? Decide whether the dragon looks evil or friendly and talk about what his plan might be. Ask: *Do you think the witch is aware that the dragon is there? Why do you think this? Why does the owl look so scared?*

- Discuss what type of story has witches and dragons and what usually happens in these stories. Invite children to recall stories with witches and dragons in them. Encourage prediction about the style and content of this book based on this prior knowledge.

- Turn to the decorative inner page and discuss the following: *Who do you think the hat, wand,*

broom and bow belong to? What do you think has happened to the witch? What makes you think this? What time of day is it? What is the weather like? (look at the objects in the sky for clues) Explore the illustration on the first spread. Encourage children to describe the setting and the weather from visual clues. Ask: *What part does the wind play in this part of the story?*

- Re-read the first spread together and make comparisons with poetry (for example, regular pattern, rhyming couplets, sentences starting with 'And' and 'But'). Identify the rhyming words at the end of alternate lines. Continue this comparison when exploring the second spread, where the text resembles the verses of a poem.

- Look at the illustrations of the witch together. Ask: *Does she seem a typical witch?* Count how many typical 'witch' items you can find.

- Which word does the author use to describe the sound of the broomstick flying into the air? (whoosh) Ask the children to think of different words that describe this sound (for example, 'swish', 'swoosh', 'wheee').

- Discuss what is known about the dog. Ask: *Can you find words to describe him? ('…thundering paws', 'keen') What role does he play in this section? How does his question link to the title? Does this give us a clue about future events?*

Ask the children, whenever appropriate, to revisit the text to exemplify/support the answers.

Encourage the children to read aloud back to the group when referring to the text – praise clear, confident and expressive reading.

ASSESSMENT OPPORTUNITIES

The following bank of question prompts provides a quick and easy means of monitoring the children's comprehension skills and understanding of the text. The children's answers to a question must be supported by evidence from the text.

Understanding

- Can you explain what you know about the characters from the first two spreads?

- Who is the main character? What is she like? Can you describe her personality? What is a typical witch personality? How does this witch compare?

Inferences

- How do you think the witch feels when the story starts? How do you know this? How is the cat feeling? Which two words on the first page describe the characters' feelings? ('purred', 'grinned')
- How do you think the witch feels as she searches for her hat? Do her feelings change when the dog finds it for her? How do you know these things?
- Why do you think the witch pulled her hat 'firmly down' on her head?

Predicting

- What role do you think the dragon will have in the story?
- What part do you think the strong wind will play in the story? What makes you think this?
- What do you think the next part of the story will be about?

Main ideas

- What is the main event in this section of the story?

Language, structure and presentation

- How do you know that this story is written like a poem?
- Can you describe the patterns in the way the words are organised?
- How does the story begin? Can you think of story language the author could have used to start the story?
- What is your favourite adjective in this section? Can you think of a different one with a similar meaning to use instead?
- Why has the author chosen verbs such as 'clambered', 'grinned', 'purred', 'wailed' and 'spat'? Try matching these verbs to words with similar meaning, for example, clambered/climbed. Which one sounds the best in this context? Does substituting words affect the structure of the verses? Has the author used any verbs you think are really effective? Why do you think that?

- Can you explain what the author means by 'thundering paws'? Can you think of a different adjective to use to describe the dog's paws?
- Which sounds best in a story or poem, 'There bounded a dog' or 'A dog ran in'? Which do you prefer for this story and why?
- How does the author change the words 'wild' and 'firm' into adverbs that describe how the wind blew and the witch pulled down her hat? Can you spot any more adverbs in this section? ('eagerly', 'politely')

Themes and conventions

- Is this a fiction or non-fiction book? How do you know?
- What clues can you find about the type of story this is from exploring the cover and reading this section? (fantasy tale)

SESSION AIMS

Discussing the sequence of events and how items of information are related.

READ

- Ask the children to read the next three spreads (3 to 5) independently. Invite them to consider some of these questions:
  - What is the main event in this section?
  - How is this section of the story similar to the first two spreads? Were your predictions about what would happen correct?
  - What does the witch lose? How does she come to lose this item?
  - Which new character appears in this section? What does she do?
  - Which words describe the setting in this section?

During reading

- While children are reading, emphasise the need to check that the text makes sense to them, particularly as they tackle unfamiliar or difficult words. Respond to individuals with praise and encouragement for confident reading.

REVIST AND RESPOND

Bring the group back together and discuss some of the points below.

Note: Since there are only 20 minutes for each session, you are advised to focus on only one or two of the elements that are listed below.

- Explore the illustration on spread 3. What are the dog and the cat staring at? Look at their expressions. How do the children think they feel? Focus on the expression on the face of the witch, which is much more cheerful. Ask: *Why do you think her expression is different? What do the animals know that the witch has yet to find out?* (Her bow has blown away.) *Why do you think the witch is holding her hat? What happened to it in the first part of the story?* Read the text on this spread together. Ask: *Which words give clues about the setting? Which phrases show that the dog and the witch are happy as the section begins?*

- Read spread 4 together. Ask the children what they notice about the way it is organised. Compare this with the text on spread 2. Find words, phrases and punctuation marks that are repeated in both. Talk about whether this regular pattern helps us to predict the way the next section will look. Identify the question that the dog and the bird ask and the way the rhyme is repeated in the words they speak.

- Discuss the use of brackets to give additional information on spread 4. Ask: *What extra information are we given inside them?* Ask the children to find the sets of speech marks. Who is speaking each time and how do they know? Why do they think the bird is asking if there is room on the broom? Does a bird need to ride on a broom?

- Read spread 5 together. Talk about the expression 'the back of beyond'. What sort of place do the children think this might be? Ask: *What did the witch do that made her lose her wand? Which do you think is more important to her, the bow or the wand? Why do you think this?*

- Explore the author's choice of descriptive language, for example, to describe the bird's movement ('flapped', 'fluttered'). Ask children to find the adjective that describes the wind ('stormy'). Why do they think the author has chosen the word 'shot' to describe the movement of the broomstick through the sky? Identify the adjectives that the dog in the earlier spreads and the bird in this section use to describe themselves ('keen', 'green'). What do the children notice about these words? Encourage them to comment on other words they particularly like.

- Talk about what might happen next. *Who do you think will be the next character to appear? Why do you think this?*

Ask the children, whenever appropriate, to revisit the text to exemplify/support the answers.

Encourage the children to read aloud back to the group when referring back to the text – praise clear, confident and expressive reading.

ASSESSMENT OPPORTUNITIES

The following bank of question prompts provides a quick and easy means of monitoring the children's comprehension skills and understanding of the text. The children's answers to a question must be supported by evidence from the text.

Understanding

- Can you explain what has happened in this section? What is similar and what is different about this section and the first section that you read?
- What clue can you find about the time of year? (ripe cornfields)
- Have you ever lost one of your belongings? Did you find it yourself, or did someone find it for you? How did you feel when you lost it/found it again?

Inferences

- What has changed in the seating arrangements on the broomstick as it flies through the rain? Why do you think the cat has moved next to the dog? Why are they clinging on to each other? What is the witch clinging on to? Which character is the only happy one? Find a phrase to prove this in the text. ('The bird shrieked with glee.')
- Which character interests you the most and why?

Predicting

- Can you find a clue in the small illustration of the wand falling into the river that tells you who might find the lost wand for the witch?
- Do you think there will be room for any more characters on the broom?
- What do you think might happen if the broom gets too full?

Language, structure and presentation

- Which two rhyming sentences are your favourites and why do you like them?
- Can you find a sentence that also appeared in the first two spreads?
- Which adjectives does the author use to describe the wind/plait/bird? Can you think of a different adjective to put in front of each noun to change the meaning; for example, 'calm wind'?

- Can you explain what the author means by 'ear-splitting shriek'? Can you think of other words to describe this sound?
- Which sounds best in a story or poem, 'There flapped a green bird' or 'A green bird flew past'? Which do you prefer for this story and why?

Themes and conventions

- What can you see that suggests that this is a fairy/fantasy tale? (castle)
- What evidence of magic is there in this section? (The witch tapped her broomstick with her wand and whoosh!)

SESSION 3: DISASTER STRIKES!

SESSION AIMS

Making inferences on the basis of what has been read so far.

READ

- Ask the children to read spreads 6 to 8, thinking about some of the following questions:
  - Which two new characters appear in this section?
  - Can you say two important things the frog did that changed the story?
  - Which words describe the setting in this section? How do the illustrations help you to imagine this landscape?
  - What do you think happened to the animals after they fell into the bog?

During reading

- Listen closely to individuals while they read and praise them for clear, confident diction. Comment positively on appropriate variation in expression and predictions related to future events.

REVISIT AND RESPOND

Bring the group back together and discuss some of the points below, focusing on spreads 6, 7 and 8.

Note: Since there are only 20 minutes for each session, you are advised to focus on only one or two of the elements that are listed below.

- Compare the expressions on the characters' faces on the broomstick on spreads 6 and 7. How do the children think they feel before and after the broom snaps? Ask: *Have you ever been doing something you enjoyed when something happened to spoil this enjoyment? Think of words to describe your changing feelings.* Look at the small illustration of the witch flying into a cloud and read the words underneath. Ask the children what the witch could be imagining here.

- Explore the illustrations of the dragon and read the text alongside. Ask: *Does he seem like a typical story-book dragon? What does he plan to do? Do you think he is good or evil? What makes you think this? How many words can you think of to describe him?*

- Explore the punctuation. What extra information is given inside the brackets? Talk about information that was given in brackets previously and notice that it has been something about the witch in all three sections. Recall the use of an ellipsis, or explain if children are unfamiliar with this. Ask the children to read the words before and after each ellipsis in this section, pausing dramatically for effect before delivering the shock words that follow. Talk about why the author uses exclamation marks as well as capital letters for certain words. Read these sentences with extra emphasis where indicated. Find the sets of speech marks and identify the speakers. Ask the children to read the words using appropriate voices. Ask: *What do you think the frog's croaking voice sounds like? How will it compare to the dragon's roaring?*

- Explore the use of descriptive words. Ask: *Why has the author chosen the word 'tumbling' instead of 'falling' to describe the movement of the animals through the sky?* Compare their movement to the movement of clothes in a tumble dryer. *Why do you think the words 'dripping wet' are repeated twice to describe both the wand and frog?* Ask children to imagine the frog emerging triumphantly from the pond holding the wand aloft. Why does the author use the word 'clean' to describe the frog, and 'mean' to describe the dragon? Point out how these words link to previous words for the dog and bird, 'keen' and 'green'. The frog 'bounded' onto the broomstick. *Which animal in a previous section* bounded? *Do you think this word is a good choice to describe the bouncing movements of these creatures?*

- Explain that the next section that you read will be the end of the story. Ask children how they think it will finish. Encourage them to talk about what they think will happen to the witch, the animals and the dragon, and to give reasons.

Ask the children, whenever appropriate, to revisit the text to exemplify/support the answers.

Encourage the children to read aloud back to the group when referring back to the text – praise clear, confident and expressive reading.

ASSESSMENT OPPORTUNITIES

The following bank of question prompts provides a quick and easy means of monitoring the children's comprehension skills and understanding of the text. The children's answers to a question must be supported by evidence from the text.

Understanding

- Can you explain what has happened in this section? What is different about this section and the earlier sections that you read?
- What is the dragon planning to have for tea?
- Up until now the witch has answered 'Yes!' to every question asked. What does she shout to the dragon when he says he wants witch for tea?
- How do you think the witch felt when the dragon flew after her? Can you explain how it feels to be scared?
- Why couldn't the witch cast a spell on the dragon to make him go away?
- Which sentence shows that the dragon was very hungry and could not wait to eat the witch?

Inferences

- The witch shouted for help when the dragon chased her. Why did no one answer?
- What do you think the witch is thinking as she falls to the ground and looks up at the dragon?
- Can you find a clue in a small picture that shows what the dragon likes to eat?
- Which is your favourite part of this section?

Predicting

- Do you think the other animals will come back and, if so, when?
- How could the witch mend her broom?
- Where do you think her wand is?
- How does the last sentence on spread 8 make you feel? Are you eager to find out what happens next?

Language, structure and presentation

- Which is your favourite sentence? What do you like about it?
- Which animal do these words describe: 'dripping wet', 'polite', 'croak', 'clean', 'bounded' and 'roar', 'scary', 'loud', 'breathing fire', 'licking lips'?
- Why does the author use capital letters for some words when characters are speaking? What does this tell you about how to read these words?

Themes and conventions

- Which new character suggests that this is a fairy/ fantasy tale? (the dragon)
- This author often writes in rhyme. Do you like her style? Why?
- What do you like most about the illustrations in this section? How do they add to your enjoyment of the story?

▼ SESSION 4: THE POWER OF FRIENDSHIP

Explaining their understanding.

READ

- Ask the children to read the final four spreads independently. Invite them to consider some of these questions:
  - Can you name all the characters that appear in this final section?
  - What happens when the beast appears?
  - What happens after the dragon flies away?
  - What is special about the new broom?
  - What happens at the end of the story?

During reading

- Give praise to those who tackle new or difficult words with confidence. Positively comment on individuals who demonstrate a good understanding of the content.

REVISIT AND RESPOND

Bring the group back together and discuss some of the points below, which cover the final four spreads (9 to 12).

Note: Since there are only 20 minutes for each session, you are advised to focus on only one or two of the elements that are listed below.

- Focus on spread 9 and ask: *What does the beast look like? Which words in the text provide extra information about its appearance? How can you tell that the animals have created the beast themselves? Why does it have four heads? Why is it tall? Which animals are responsible for the feathers, fur and wings? What props have they used?* (broomstick and cauldron) *Why is the beast dark and sticky? Which four words describe how the beast sounds? Which animals made these sounds? Can you make the noise of the beast?* (Ask the children to choose different sounds and make the noise in unison.)

- If you had a discussion in the last session about whether the dragon is good or evil, ask if the children feel the same about him now. Provide them with antonyms and ask which they would use to describe the dragon: for example, brave/cowardly, strong/weak, fierce/timid. Do the children think he reacted like a typical dragon when he saw the beast?

- Re-read spreads 11 and 12 and talk about how the animals helped the witch to create the new broom. Ask: *How was it possible for the witch to do magic again? If you could cast a spell for something 'truly magnificent', what would you choose? Look at the illustration of the new broom. Why do you think it is described as truly magnificent? Which part do you like best and why? If you could add something, what would it be?*

- Find the sets of speech marks throughout the final four spreads. Ask the children to read '"Buzz off! – THAT'S MY WITCH!"' using all the techniques indicated by the punctuation and earlier information about the sounds. Read the dragon's speech together. Ask children to recall any previous voices they used and to decide whether the dragon's words should be said in this voice. Ask: *How do you think the dragon is feeling now? Think of words to describe his mood. How will his voice sound now?* Read his words in this voice. Discuss how the witch feels grateful after being rescued. Read her speech in a lively, excited, happy way… but remember to mutter the spell with emphasis on the word 'ZOOM' as indicated!

- Explore descriptive words. Why has the author chosen 'strode' instead of 'walked' to describe the beast as it emerged from the ditch? Let the children have fun miming the difference between these words (for example, suggest that children form a group of four, hanging on to one another, and moving in unison).

- Have a discussion about the ending of the story. Ask: *Do you think this is a good ending? Would you have changed it in any way? Where do you think the characters will fly to next on their new broom? Where would you fly to?*

Ask the children, whenever appropriate, to revisit the text to exemplify/support the answers.

Encourage the children to read aloud back to the group when referring back to the text – praise clear, confident and expressive reading.

ASSESSMENT OPPORTUNITIES

The following bank of question prompts provides a quick and easy means of monitoring the children's comprehension skills and understanding of the text. The children's answers to a question must be supported by evidence from the text.

Understanding

• Can you describe how the animals constructed the beast? Who was near the top? Who was at the bottom?

• Did things happen as you predicted? Was anything unexpected?

• How did the animals prove that they were good friends of the witch? Do you think their plan to scare the dragon worked?

• What was on the new broom especially for each character?

Inferences

• What was the *'feast'* the dragon planned to have at the start of this section?

• What made the dragon shake and why did he fly off?

• Do you think that the witch knew it was her friends pretending to be the beast? How would that make her feel?

• Why does the witch say she would be inside the dragon without her friends' help?

• What did you like best in this section? Can you say why?

Predicting

• What do you think will happen to the dragon?

• Will the friends stay together for further adventures?

• The last sentence is repeated several times in the story. Do you think it is a good sentence on which to end the story? Does it make you eager to find out what happens next?

Language, structure and presentation

• Which adjectives describe the beast? Which is your favourite? Can you think of two new adjectives to use?

• The author uses interesting verbs to describe how creatures move and speak. Can you mime these movements? 'The beast rose', 'The dragon spluttered', 'They all clambered'.

• Which sounds best in a story or poem, 'Down flew the bird, down jumped the frog' or 'The bird flew down, The frog jumped down?' Which do you prefer for this story and why?

Themes and conventions

• What does the witch do to make the new broom? How is this typical of a fairy/fantasy tale?

• Why are friends so important in this story? In what ways are your friends important to you?

▼ SESSION 1: SETTING THE SCENE

SESSION AIMS

Meeting the characters and setting the scene.

READ

- Look at the front cover of the book and read the title. Ask the children to locate the lighthouse, the lighthouse keeper and the lunch. Ask:
  - Why do you think the lighthouse keeper looks so grumpy?
  - What do you think the main idea of this story might be?
  - Where is the story set?
  - Why might a lighthouse be an interesting setting for a story? What problems could there be?
- Ask volunteers to read the first four spreads aloud.

During reading

- Move around the group and 'tune in' to hear individuals read aloud. Encourage and praise good expression.

REVISIT AND RESPOND

Bring the group back together and discuss some of the points below, focusing on the first four spreads.

Note: Since there are only 20 minutes for each session, you are advised to focus on only one or two of the elements that are listed below.

- Review any unfamiliar vocabulary from the first four spreads. Discuss the meaning of 'perched', 'polish', 'industrious', 'tended' and 'concocting', encouraging the children to use the context and illustrations to make a suggestion. Help the children to understand that 'perched' makes the house sound like it was right on the edge of something very steep, that 'tended' makes it sound as if Mr Grinling looks after the lighthouse with great care and 'concocting' suggests that Mrs Grinling uses lots of imagination in putting together Mr Grinling's lunch.
- Talk about the setting of the story. Allow time for the children to talk about their experiences of being at the seaside and any lighthouses or rocky cliffs

they've seen. Challenge them to look through this section and find opposites. (the sea and the land; the bad weather and the sunny weather; the house and the lighthouse; the day and the night) Ask the children to describe Mr Grinling's journey to work in the mornings. What do they think he does when the weather is bad? Do they think he ever gets stuck on land or at the lighthouse?

- Discuss Mr Grinling's job. Ask: *Why does he clean and polish the light every day? What would happen if he didn't?* Talk about the role of lighthouses and explain the importance of ships knowing where rocks are in the dark. Look at the second spread. Will Mr Grinling have particular problems to face in these different conditions? Think about the expression on his face – is he happy or sad?

- Ask the children to think about the characters of Mr and Mrs Grinling and discuss them in pairs. What sort of person do they think Mr Grinling is? Look together for clues in the story so far. Ask: *What does Mr Grinling think about in bed at night? What does this tell us about him?* What sort of person do the children think Mrs Grinling is? Encourage them to look for clues in the story and the illustrations. How do the characters feel in this part of the story? Look at the expressions on the faces of Mr and Mrs Grinling on these pages. Even the cat is smiling. Compare the characters' faces here with Mr Grinling's face on the cover.

- Look together at spread 4. Point out that up to this point the book has been about the lighthouse keeper – now we have the lunch itself. (Remind the children of the title of the book if necessary.) Ask: *How does Mrs Grinling send Mr Grinling his lunch? Do you think this is a good idea? Why doesn't Mr Grinling take lunch with him?* (Perhaps, Mrs Grinling wants to make fresh and special food.) *Why doesn't he row home for lunch?* (There are an awful lot of steps. Perhaps it would take too long. Sending the basket on the zip wire seems to work.)

- Look at the picture of Mrs Grinling in her kitchen. Ask: *What is she making?* (peach surprise) *List the ingredients. How long might it take to make? When will it be ready?* (Note that the time is 11.30 on the clock.)

THE LIGHTHOUSE KEEPER'S LUNCH ▼

Ask the children, whenever appropriate, to revisit the text to exemplify/support the answers.

Encourage the children to read aloud back to the group when referring back to the text – praise clear, confident and expressive reading.

ASSESSMENT OPPORTUNITIES

The following bank of question prompts provides a quick and easy means of monitoring the children's comprehension skills and understanding of the text. The children's answers to a question must be supported by evidence from the text.

Understanding
* When does Mr Grinling clean the lighthouse light?
* What is perched high on the cliffs?
* When do the ships toot to Mr Grinling?
* Where is Mrs Grinling in the morning while Mr Grinling is polishing his light?
* What ingredients does Mrs Grinling use in the peach surprise recipe?

Inferences
* What is Mr Grinling's main task as a lighthouse keeper? How do you know that?
* Is Mr Grinling a hard-working lighthouse keeper? Explain how you know this.
* Why do you think Mr Grinling goes to work without taking his lunch with him?
* Is Mr Grinling a happy man most of the time? What reason do you have for saying that?
* What do you think Mrs Grinling might have packed in the lunch basket? Why do you say that?
* How does Mrs Grinling feel about making the lunch each day? Why do you think that?
* Why do you think that the ships 'tell him that his light was shining brightly and clearly out to sea'?

Predicting
* What do you think is going to happen to the lunch?

Main ideas
* How would you describe the story so far – happy or sad?

Language, structure and presentation
* Mrs Grinling spends each morning 'concocting a delicious lunch'. What do you think the word 'concocting' means here?
* Suggest another word for 'delicious'.
* What does the word 'tended' say about how Mr Grinling looks after his light?

SESSION AIMS

Meeting the characters and setting the scene.

READ

- This session focuses on spreads 5 to 7. Ask the children to tell you the story so far, remembering how happy Mr and Mrs Grinling have been up to this point and how successful their lunch system seems to be.

- Ask volunteers to read aloud up to spread 7, telling the children to think about the following questions as they listen:
  - What does Mrs Grinling make for lunch?
  - On what day of the week did the seagulls first eat Mr Grinling's lunch?
  - What is Mrs Grinling's plan for protecting the lunch on Tuesday? Does it work?
  - How do the seagulls get to the lunch?
  - What did Mr Grinling do when he saw the seagulls eat his lunch?

During reading
- Talk about the meaning of unfamiliar words as they come up, encouraging the children to try to tackle them themselves.

REVISIT AND RESPOND

Bring the group back together and discuss some of the points below, focusing on the first four spreads.

Note: Since there are only 20 minutes for each session, you are advised to focus on only one or two of the elements that are listed below.

- Discuss the descriptive language used by the author on spreads 5 to 7: 'particularly', 'appetising', 'garni', 'scavenging', 'devoured', 'gusto', 'varmints', 'scrumptious', 'baffle' and 'sound plan'. Read some of the sentences again, replacing the tricky words with more straightforward vocabulary: for example, 'appetising' with 'tasty', 'devoured' with 'ate','scrumptious' with 'really nice'. Ask the children which version of the sentences they prefer and why.

Ask them to tell the rest of the group which is their favourite new word out of these and which they might try to use in the future.

- Look at the fifth spread, showing the food that Mrs Grinling has made Mr Grinling for lunch. Discuss the different dishes and speculate on the ingredients. Talk about which of the dishes the children would like to eat. Ask any children in the group who have packed lunches to compare their usual lunch with Mr Grinling's lunch. Which would they prefer to eat? Agree that Mrs Grinling seems to have prepared an enormous feast! Tell the children to describe their ultimate lunch to a partner. Share the children's menus. Return to spread 5 and ask questions such as: *Do you think it a healthy lunch? Which dish from the lunch would you like to try? Why is seafood salad a good dish for a lighthouse keeper? What do you think is in the seafood salad? If you were making a Lighthouse Sandwich, what would you put in it?*

- Talk about the seagulls on spreads 6 and 7. What adjectives can the children think of to describe the character of the seagulls? (perhaps: 'cheeky', 'naughty', 'arrogant', 'brave', 'rude'.) Share any stories that the children have of seagulls stealing their picnic. What do they think of the seagulls in this story?

- Ask the children to take on the roles of the different seagulls and have a go at putting on voices for them. Ask: *How can we capture a seagull-y sound?* Let the children have fun acting out the dialogue on spread 6, perhaps with one child in the role of Mr Grinling. Share ideas on what the seagulls might be thinking. Ask: *What do the seagulls think of the food? What do they think of Mr Grinling? Why don't the seagulls fly away when Mr Grinling shouts at them?*

- Consider how the characters of Mr and Mrs Grinling are developing. Remind the children how happy Mr and Mrs Grinling (and their cat) were in the first pages of the story. Compare one of the earlier spreads with the image of him shouting at the birds from the lighthouse. Tell the children to look at his face. Ask: *How does Mr Grinling feel now? How do we know?* Move on to spread 7 and ask: *How does Mrs Grinling feel? Why is she smiling?* (possibly because she thinks she has a cunning plan)

Ask the children, whenever appropriate, to revisit the text to exemplify/support the answers.

Encourage the children to read aloud back to the group when referring back to the text – praise clear, confident and expressive reading.

ASSESSMENT OPPORTUNITIES

The following bank of question prompts provides a quick and easy means of monitoring the children's comprehension skills and understanding of the text. The children's answers to a question must be supported by evidence from the text.

Understanding

- What is the terrible thing that happens on Monday?
- What sort of salad does Mrs Grinling make?
- How many savoury dishes does Mrs Grinling make for lunch?
- List four other dishes that Mrs Grinling makes for Mr Grinling's lunch on Monday.
- What does the seagull (on spread 7) say to the other gulls?
- What is the sound plan Mr Grinling agrees to?

Inferences

- Why do you think Mrs Grinling makes so much lunch for her husband?
- How does Mr Grinling feel when the seagulls steal his lunch? Why do you say that?
- Do you think that it is fair for the gulls to eat Mr Grinling's lunch? Explain why you think that.
- Are the seagulls scared of Mr Grinling? How do you know that?
- Do you think Mr and Mrs Grinling's plan is a good one?
- When is the napkin tied to the basket? Explain how you know.
- Bonus question! As a final challenge for text detectives: what is Mr Grinling's first name?

Language, structure and presentation

- Cold Chicken Garni is one of the foods in the basket. Look at the picture and explain what you think 'Garni' is.
- Explain what you think is meant by 'Assorted Fruit'.
- What does the author mean by 'scavenging seagulls'?
- Explain the meaning of 'devoured with great gusto'.
- Think of a word that means the opposite to scrumptious.
- What is your favourite phrase from these pages?

Themes and conventions

- Who is cleverer – Mrs Grinling or the seagulls?

▼ SESSION 3: HAMISH TO THE RESCUE

SESSION AIMS

Making inferences and predictions.

READ

- Ask the children to help you remember what has happened in the story so far. Remind them that the seagulls ate Mr Grinling's lunch on Monday and Tuesday. Read spreads 8 to 10, asking the children to bear the following questions in mind:
  - What is Mrs Grinling's plan on Tuesday evening?
  - Who is Hamish?
  - Why does Mrs Grinling think Hamish will protect the lunch?
  - What will Mrs Grinling give Hamish when he's back?
  - Why doesn't the plan work? What happens when Hamish is on the wire with the lunch?

- As you come across them, discuss the meaning of 'racked their brains', 'brazen', 'accomplished', 'guard', 'ingenious', 'secured' and 'agree' (in this context). Provide versions of the sentences with simpler vocabulary; for example, 'thought', 'brave', 'good', 'watch', 'clever', 'tied' and 'suit'. As in the last session, ask the children which they prefer – the simple or the more challenging version.

REVISIT AND RESPOND

Bring the group back together and discuss some of the points below, focusing on spreads 8 to 10.

Note: Since there are only 20 minutes for each session, you are advised to focus on only one or two of the elements that are listed below.

- Ask the children to look at the spread for Tuesday evening. Tell them to turn to a partner and describe what is going on in the left-hand scene. Share the children's ideas and encourage the group to describe the scene in as much detail as possible, including the sunset and the man fishing in the background. Discuss Hamish's thoughts about the seagulls. Ask: *Is Hamish about to pounce on the seagulls? Or is he crouching down away from the seagulls?*

- Turn to the scene on the right-hand side of spread 8. Ask: *When does this take place?* Encourage the children to visualise the scene, thinking about the sounds that might accompany it (hissing, scratching, yowling, spitting, meowing). Ask: *What does Mrs Grinling think of Hamish?* (She thinks he's brave.) Now encourage the children to infer what Hamish is really thinking. What does he think of seagulls? Do the children think he is *an accomplished seagull chaser?* Ask: *How does Hamish feel about going in the basket? How do we know? Why doesn't Hamish protect the lunch? What do the seagulls think of Hamish? How does Hamish feel on Wednesday evening?* (Hint: look for clues in the illustrations on spread 10.)

- Introduce the word 'theme' and explain that a theme is a main idea in the book. Ask: *What do you think the main idea of the book is?* (Perhaps: clever plans, or who can get the lunch.) Ask: *How would you protect the lunch from the hungry seagulls?* Tell the children to work in pairs to come up with some suggestions. As a group, discuss the different ideas that the pairs have come up with. Encourage the children to (kindly) discuss the pros and cons of each idea. (Perhaps Mr Grinling could take the lunch with him; but then Mrs Grinling would have to get up early or make less; perhaps Mrs Grinling could put everything in plastic boxes, but maybe the story is set before plastic boxes were widely available; perhaps Mrs Grinling could put an alarm clock in the basket, but the alarm might stop ringing before the basket arrives, or it may not scare the seagulls, and so on.)

- Challenge the children to predict what Mrs Grinling's final plan might be. Read the right-hand side of spread 10 for a clue. What do the children think she means by 'just the mixture for hungry seagulls'? Is she thinking about a tasty fishy snack or something horrid?

- Tell the children to compare Mr Grinling's face on spreads 8 and 10 with his face at the beginning of the story, or in his wedding photo on spread 10. How is he feeling now? Compare his expression with Mrs Grinling's. Why do the children think she remains smiling throughout the spreads? (Perhaps because she's always feeling positive about the next plan.)

Ask the children, whenever appropriate, to revisit the text to exemplify/support the answers.

Encourage the children to read aloud back to the group when referring back to the text – praise clear, confident and expressive reading.

ASSESSMENT OPPORTUNITIES

The following bank of question prompts provides a quick and easy means of monitoring the children's comprehension skills and understanding of the text. The children's answers to a question must be supported by evidence from the text.

Understanding

- Who is Mrs Grinling talking about when she says, '"They are a brazen lot…"'?
- What does Mrs Grinling say Hamish can do tomorrow?
- What does Hamish do as Mrs Grinling is trying to put him in the basket?
- What is Hamish told will be waiting for him when he arrives home?
- What happens when Hamish peers down at the sea?

Inferences

- Why do you think Mrs Grinling says, '"Our cat does not appear to like seagulls"'?
- What is Hamish's favourite food? Why do you think that?
- How do you think Hamish feels about going into the basket? Explain why you say that.
- Are the seagulls being kind to Hamish as he sits in the basket on the wire? Why do you say that?
- Are the seagulls scared of Hamish?
- What do you think Mrs Grinling is planning next? Why do you say that?

Language, structure and presentation

- Mr and Mrs Grinling racked their brains for another plan. Explain what the author means by 'racked their brains'.
- Mrs Grinling describes the seagulls as 'a brazen lot'. Is she describing them as being bold or shy here?
- Suggest another word that has the same meaning as 'accomplished'.
- What is a herring?
- Is the Grinlings' plan ingenious? Why do you say that?
- Is Mrs Grinling talking to Hamish in a consoling way? Explain how you know that.

Predicting

- How do you think the Grinlings will protect the lunch from the seagulls?

Themes and conventions

- Do you think it is a good idea to put Hamish in the basket?

▼ SESSION 4: SUCCESS AT LAST!

SESSION AIMS

Considering the significance of the ending for the different characters, and the structure of the story.

READ

- As a group, remember or read the story up to spread 10. Then read from spread 11 to the end. (Ensure that the children understand why the seagulls wouldn't like mustard sandwiches.) Prompt the children with the following questions to ensure they've understood the story:
  - Look at the mustard sandwiches. Can you explain what Mrs Grinling is planning?
  - What do you think the word 'expectant' means? What are the seagulls expecting?
  - What are Mr and Mrs Grinling expecting to happen?
  - Imagine the seagulls eating the mustard sandwiches; what sounds do they make?
  - Mrs Grinling is jubilant about the success of her plan. Is 'jubilant' happier or sadder than 'pleased'?
  - What would a sumptuous lunch be like? Would it be good to eat?
  - Where do the seagulls plan to have lunch on Sunday?
- Help the children to understand the meaning of unfamiliar vocabulary such as 'scrumptious', 'snatches of sea shanties', 'surveyed', 'chocolate éclair', 'mused', and so on. Encourage them to use the words in new sentences.

During reading

- Move around the group and 'tune in' to hear individuals read aloud. Encourage and praise good expression.

REVISIT AND RESPOND

Bring the group back together and discuss some of the points below.

Note: Since there are only 20 minutes for each session, you are advised to focus on only one or two of the elements that are listed below.

- Ask the children to recap on Mrs Grinling's different attempts to save Mr Grinling's lunch from the seagulls. Can they remember what went wrong each time? Look at spreads 11 to 13 and discuss the mustard sandwiches. Ask: *How does Mrs Grinling feel as she puts the basket of mustard sandwiches onto the zip wire? How does Hamish feel now? Why does Mrs Grinling make mustard sandwiches a second time?* Read the left-hand side of spread 13 and ask the children if the seagulls have learned their lesson. (Yes, because one says 'Let's go and have lunch elsewhere'.) Say: *Imagine the seagulls fly off and land on the cliffs. Where might they look for their lunch tomorrow?*
- Focus on the last pages of the story. Do the children think the story has a happy ending? If so, who for? Ask: *Is it a happy ending for the seagulls? What about the man in the boat?*
- Talk about the structure of the story. Ask the children to plot the action against the days of the week. Point out that the opening of the story doesn't take place on any particular day. Ask them to start plotting the story from, 'But one Monday…'.
- Look at the passing of time throughout the story. Ask the children to find words in the book that relate to time (night time, morning, one Monday, That evening, and so on). Ask: *What time of year do you think the main part of the story is set? What clues can you see?* (It is possibly summer as it is warm enough to sit outside in the evening and it looks very hot on the last spread.)

- Ask the children to sum up Mr Grinling's changing emotions in the story. Ask: *What does Mr Grinling see through his telescope? How does this make him feel?* Mr Grinling sings sea shanties as he watches the seagulls through his telescope. Explain that a sea shanty is a song made up of strong rhythms to help sailors perform repetitive tasks. Ask: *What does Mr Grinling singing tell us about how he is feeling?*

Ask the children, whenever appropriate, to revisit the text to exemplify/support the answers.

Encourage the children to read aloud back to the group when referring to the text – praise clear, confident and expressive reading.

ASSESSMENT OPPORTUNITIES

The following bank of question prompts provides a quick and easy means of monitoring the children's comprehension skills and understanding of the text. The children's answers to a question must be supported by evidence from the text.

Understanding
- What is 'extra strong'?
- When does Mrs Grinling pack the mustard sandwiches?
- Who wants to have lunch elsewhere?
- What does Mrs Grinling do before she prepares Mr Grinling's lunch on Saturday?
- What does Mr Grinling do as he waits for his lunch?

Inferences
- Why do you think Mr Grinling chuckles about the mustard sandwiches?
- Does Mrs Grinling rush to pack the sandwiches? How do you know that?
- Do you think Hamish and Mrs Grinling are expecting the seagulls to react badly to the sandwiches? Why do you think that?

- How do you think the seagulls feel after they've taken the first bite of the mustard sandwiches?
- Does Mrs Grinling repeat the mustard mixture on Saturday? How do you know that?
- Where are the seagulls planning to have lunch the next day? Explain how you know.
- How do you think Mr Grinling feels after he has looked through his telescope? Why do you think that?

Language, structure and presentation
- How is the story organised?
- Find three phrases in the story that tell you when the events are taking place.
- What are sea shanties?
- Mr Grinling sings 'snatches of sea shanties'. Explain what the word 'snatches' means here.
- Mr Grinling 'surveyed' the coastline. What does the author mean by this?
- Did you like the tricky words in this book? Which word will you try to use in the next story you write?

Main ideas
- Did you enjoy the story? What was your favourite part? Explain why you liked it.
- What might happen to the Grinlings on another adventure?

Themes and conventions
- Who is cleverer in the end: the seagulls or Mrs Grinling?
- Did you expect Mrs Grinling to find a way to protect the lunch?

▼ SESSION 1: MEETING WINNIE AND WILBUR

SESSION AIMS

Discussing the significance of the title and opening pages.

READ

- Ask the children to look at the front and back covers of the book and think about the following:
  - What does the front cover show?
  - What might this tell us about what will happen in the book?
  - What does the blurb on the back cover tell us?
  - From this, what might the story be about?

- If children find it difficult to read the text on the back cover, read it aloud to them. After they have done this, ask them to read the first two spreads in the book independently, bearing in mind their thoughts on the covers.

REVISIT AND RESPOND

Bring the group back together and discuss some of the points below, which relate to the covers and the first two spreads.

Note: Since there are only 20 minutes for each session, you are advised to focus on only one or two of the elements that are listed below.
Ask questions about the covers: *What is happening to Winnie on the stairs on the front cover? Why is she falling over? What expressions do she and Wilbur have on their faces? What might the covers (front and back) tell you about what the story might be about?* (Winnie falling over Wilbur and the trouble this causes.)

- Look at the first spread together and ask the children which adjective is repeated. How many times is the adjective written down? (The adjective is 'black' and it is repeated nine times.) Ask the children why the author chose to do this, rather than just list the items and say they were all black. (The repetition emphasises just how black everything is.) Ask them: *Would you like to live in a house where everything was black?*

- Consider Winnie and how she is dressed. Ask the children how she stands out from the rest of the house, and to describe her clothing. (She dresses very colourfully, with a blue dress, a purple jacket or cardigan, stripy yellow and orange tights, and so on.) Is this how witches usually dress? How are witches often portrayed in other stories they have read? (Often, witches are shown wearing black, not colour.) Why do the children think Winnie wears colours but has such a dark house and belongings?

- Consider the title of the story. Why is it called *Winnie the Witch*? Why isn't Wilbur mentioned in the title, and do the children think that this has a bearing on what will happen in the story? From her appearance, what do they think Winnie is like as a person? How does she compare to witches they have read or heard about in other stories, such as fairy tales?

- Read out the blurb on the back cover and ask the children what they think Winnie will use her magic to do, if she needs to make sure she can always see Wilbur…? Ask: *Why is there an ellipsis after those words?* (It hints that this will be what the story is about and possibly that the magic might not be very helpful at all!)

- Ask the children to look at the house again on both spreads and discuss and describe what it looks like, without using the word 'black'. They should focus on developing their descriptive language, commenting on the shape of things, how tidy or messy the house is. What unusual items can they spot in the pictures that they wouldn't find in their own houses (for example, a pot of worms, snakes, lizards, skulls, and so on)?

- Ask the children, whenever appropriate, to revisit the text to support their answers. Encourage them to read aloud to the group when referring back to the text – praise clear, confident and expressive reading.

Ask the children, whenever appropriate, to revisit the text to exemplify/support the answers.

Encourage the children to read aloud back to the group when referring to the text – praise clear, confident and expressive reading.

ASSESSMENT OPPORTUNITIES

The following bank of question prompts provides a quick and easy means of monitoring the children's comprehension skills and understanding of the text. The children's answers to a question must be supported by evidence from the text.

Understanding
- Name the items hanging on the washing line on the first spread.
- What colour are Wilbur's eyes?
- What is Winnie looking through on the first spread?
- Which colours are her tights?
- Where is Winnie's house located?
- What two items can you see on her hat?
- What is Winnie doing on the second spread?
- Name a few of the things you can see in her kitchen.

Inferences
- How does Winnie feel as she falls over? What about Wilbur?
- Why does Wilbur sit on her feet and legs on the second spread?
- Why does Winnie choose to live in a house where everything is black?
- What sort of book is Winnie reading?

Predicting
- What does it mean when it says, 'And that is how the trouble began?' What trouble might this refer to?
- What might Winnie do to stop the trouble?

Language, structure and presentation
- On the first spread, why does the author repeat the word 'black' nine times? What effect is she trying to achieve?
- How does the front cover suggest what might happen later in the story?

Themes and conventions
- What do the children think about always having everything in the same colour? Why might this be a bad thing? What is their favourite colour, and would they choose to have everything in their room in that colour if they could?

SESSION 2: CLAWS AND EFFECT

SESSION AIMS

Discussing the sequence of events in books and how items of information are related.

READ

- Ask the children to read spreads 3 to 7 independently. As they do, they should keep the following questions in mind:
    - Why can't Winnie see Wilbur when his eyes are closed?
    - How do Winnie and Wilbur feel when she sits, trips or falls on him?
    - What could Winnie do to stop this from happening?
    - Is magic the answer?

During reading

- Move around the group and listen to each child read aloud. Encourage and praise good expression. Encourage children to tackle difficult words by 're-running for meaning'.

REVISIT AND RESPOND

Bring the group back together and discuss some of the points below.

Note: Since there are only 20 minutes for each session, you are advised to focus on only one or two of the elements that are listed below.

- In spreads 3 and 4, and half of 5, we discover what happens when Winnie can't see Wilbur. Ask the children to look at Winnie's and Wilbur's expressions and reactions and say how both characters are feeling. In spread 4, Wilbur's expression is sly and cheeky so you could ask: *Did Wilbur mean to trip Winnie up?*

- When discussing these spreads, ask the children: *Do you think that Wilbur is as important a character as Winnie? Why or why not?* Answers could include 'yes', because what he does in response to Winnie drives the story forward as much as her awful magic. A 'no' answer might mention the fact that it is Winnie who does most of the main action and he is

in her power. Ask them why his name is not in the title, if he is an equally important character.

- In spread 6, there are two panels on the left-hand page and a whole panel on the right. The two panels on the left help to show different situations where Wilbur can be seen properly now that Winnie has cast this spell (this is rather like a pictorial 'list' with the thin white line acting as a comma). Ask the children why more space might be given to the scene on the bed (perhaps because Wilbur is doing something naughty). You could extend this activity to look at how the illustrator has split the action over the previous spreads and what effect that has on the narration of the story.

- In spread 7, the illustrator has chosen to split the page horizontally rather than vertically. Point out this difference to the children and ask them why this might be. (Perhaps it was a better choice for showing Wilbur being put out of the house and then Winnie tripping over him.) Ask the children how the illustrator shows how many times Winnie somersaults through the air (three blue circles painted onto the white background).

- Ask the children: *Do you think that Winnie is good at magic?* In particular, refer them to the right-hand page of spread 5, where she has turned Wilbur green. Did she mean to do this? If so, do they think that this was a good idea? Do they like him better in green? What colour would they have turned Wilbur? Ask: *Do you think the spell hurt him in any way?*

- Look through spreads 3 to 7 again and note down the things that are in colour, apart from Winnie's clothes and Wilbur's eyes (examples could include: yellow snakes' eyes, green frogs' legs, green plants, an orange drink on the bedside table). Ask the children why they think these items are not in black like the rest of Winnie's house.

Ask the children, whenever appropriate, to revisit the text to exemplify/support the answers.

Encourage the children to read aloud back to the group when referring back to the text – praise clear, confident and expressive reading.

ASSESSMENT OPPORTUNITIES

The following bank of question prompts provides a quick and easy means of monitoring the children's comprehension skills and understanding of the text. The children's answers to a question must be supported by evidence from the text.

Understanding

- When did Winnie sit on Wilbur?

- Where was Wilbur sitting when Winnie tripped over him?

- What does the word nasty mean in 'after a nasty fall'?

- What magic word does Winnie say to turn Wilbur green?

Inferences

- Why is Winnie carrying a net on spread 4?

- Who are the portraits of on the walls?

- Do you think Winnie injured herself when she fell down the stairs?

- How do you think Wilbur feels when he is turned green?

- Why is Wilbur not allowed to sleep on the bed?

- Why is there a ladder leaning against Winnie's bed?

- Why is the word 'Abracadabra' written differently to the normal text and why is it larger?

Predicting

- Do you think that Winnie will keep Wilbur green from now on?

Language, structure and presentation

- In spreads 3 and 4, the following phrases are repeated: 'When Wilbur sat on the…with his eyes open', 'Winnie could see him', 'She could see his eyes, anyway', 'But when Wilbur closed his eyes and went to sleep', 'Winnie couldn't see him at all. So she…'. Ask the children why these expressions are repeated nearly word for word (to show cause and effect). Repeat this question with spread 6, where phrases are also repeated.

- On spread 5, the author uses two exclamation marks in the main text and one after the 'Abracadabra' in the picture. Ask the children: *Why has the author used exclamation marks in these places?*

- On spread 7, the author splits up the sentences: '*… so Winnie put him outside. Outside in the grass'.* Ask the children why she does this rather than say 'she put him outside on the grass' in one sentence (the repetition and singling out of grass hints at the next problem).

SESSION 3: HOW ARE THEY FEELING?

SESSION AIMS

Making inferences on what is being said and done.

READ

- Ask the children to read spreads 8 to 10 independently, bearing in mind the following questions:
  - Why is Winnie so angry?
  - Is it Wilbur's fault that Winnie keeps falling over him?
  - Why is Wilbur sad?
  - How does Winnie feel about what she's done?

During reading:

- As the children read, 'tune in' to hear individuals read aloud. Remind children of the importance of understanding what they are reading and offer praise when they attempt unfamiliar words.

REVISIT AND RESPOND

Bring the group back together and discuss some of the points below, which focus on spreads 8 to 10.

Note: Since there are only 20 minutes for each session, you are advised to focus on only one or two of the elements that are listed below.

- In these spreads, the author tells us a little about Winnie's and Wilbur's emotions. Make a note of the adjectives used ('furious', 'miserable', 'worried') and ask the children if they know what the words mean. Then, ask them to give you synonyms that could be used instead of these words. Examples could include: 'furious' – angry, enraged, irate, seething; 'miserable' – sad, dejected, unhappy, glum; 'worried' – concerned, anxious, troubled, uneasy. Next, ask the children: *Which shows Winnie's and Wilbur's emotions more clearly – the words or the pictures?*
- Ask the children to look at spread 8. How has the illustrator conveyed how furious Winnie is? (Her red nose is even redder, her mouth is open wide showing her sharp, pointed teeth, and the colours

also look as if they have been splashed on violently.) How is Wilbur reacting to her fury? Do they feel sorry for Wilbur?

- Ask the children to look at spread 9 and comment on how Wilbur is feeling, from the way he is drawn. (Wilbur looks dejected with his wobbly whiskers, ears pointing slightly downwards and his droopy tail. His expression – especially around the eyes and mouth – looks sad.) Ask the children why the author says nothing about how Wilbur is feeling and only comments on his appearance and the fact that Winnie is able to see him anywhere now. (We are meant to infer his feelings from the illustrations.) Ask: *Why is Wilbur so sad?*

- Look at spread 10 and ask the children: *Why does Wilbur climb to the top of the tallest tree?* (It could be to get as far away from Winnie as possible!) Discuss why the birds are not frightened of him – most would be scared of a cat. Is it because he is so funny-looking? Why do they laugh at him? You could then relate Wilbur's experience to the children's, asking: *Has anyone ever laughed at you for something you wore or something you did? How did you feel? Did anything make you feel better? Why did Wilbur stay in the tree all night?*

- Focus on Winnie's behaviour on spreads 9 and 10. Does she look happy with what she has done? On spread 9, she is looking at Wilbur in the tree, so we cannot see her expression, but you might like to ask what she is doing and how she is feeling about Wilbur being in the tree. On spread 10, though, she looks very upset. Ask the children for evidence of this (her shoulders are hunched over, her expression is very miserable).

- Ask the children if they can think of other ways Winnie might have solved the problem, rather than turning Wilbur into different colours. For example, could she have put a coloured collar on him? Could she just have been more careful when she was walking around the house? List some ideas, including any magical spells that might have been better!

- To introduce an element of philosophy, you could ask the children if they think that what Winnie did to Wilbur was a form of mistreatment or cruelty. (You might have to explain what this is first.) Ask the children to justify their opinions. You could broaden this out to consider things like people putting their dogs into outfits, and so on. Is that unkind?

Ask the children, whenever appropriate, to revisit the text to exemplify/support the answers.

Encourage the children to read aloud back to the group when referring back to the text – praise clear, confident and expressive reading.

ASSESSMENT OPPORTUNITIES

The following bank of question prompts provides a quick and easy means of monitoring the children's comprehension skills and understanding of the text. The children's answers to a question must be supported by evidence from the text.

Understanding

- What colours are on spread 8 when Winnie waves her wand?

- How many times does Winnie wave her wand?

- What does 'furious' mean?

- What colour was Wilbur's head?

- How did the birds react when they saw Wilbur?

- How long did he stay up the tree?

Inferences

- Why was Winnie furious? Was she upset with Wilbur or with herself because her spell didn't work?

- Do you think Winnie stayed outside all night with Wilbur?

Predicting

- Will Wilbur ever come down from the tree or will Winnie have to save him?

- Do you think Wilbur will forgive Winnie for what she has done?

- Will Winnie put this situation right? What could she do?

Language, structure and presentation

- Why, on spread 8, does the author not finish the sentence, choosing instead to finish it on page 9?

- Why does the author not say how Wilbur is feeling on spread 10?

- On spread 10, the author uses two antonyms – 'loved' and 'hated' – in the same sentence. Why has she done this and what effect does this have?

Main ideas/themes and conventions

- Discuss if it is kind or cruel to change someone or something without their permission.

- Consider how you can make someone feel better when you have treated them unkindly.

▼ SESSION 4: WINNIE'S MAGIC SOLUTION

SESSION AIMS

Explaining and discussing their understanding of books.

READ

- Ask the children to read the last two spreads independently, while considering the following:
  - Why is Wilbur happy again?
  - Why does Winnie keep waving her wand over and over?
  - Will this solution be better?

During reading

- Listen to individual children as they read aloud. Encourage and praise clear, confident expression. Encourage children to tackle difficult words by thinking about the context.

REVISIT AND RESPOND

Bring the group back together and discuss some of the points below, considering the final two spreads.

Note: Since there are only 20 minutes for each session, you are advised to focus on only one or two of the elements that are listed below.

- Ask the children why the word 'Abracadabra' is much bigger on spread 11 than at all the other times. (This could be the author's way of showing that this time Winnie will be successful, or it could be to show what a big spell Winnie is casting, as she is changing much more than a cat.) Ask: What does the size of the letters suggest as to how a person should speak the word? (very loudly – it's bold and has an exclamation mark)

- Look at the left-hand page of spread 11 and ask the children why Wilbur is now happy. Has he forgiven Winnie for what she did? Where are the birds now? Would the children have forgiven Winnie so quickly for what she did? Relate what has happened to the children's experiences and ask when they have had

to forgive someone for something. Did they do it quickly or did they need time to feel less angry or upset. Ask: *Is it better to forgive someone than be angry with them for a long time?* Discuss their answers.

- On the right-hand page of spread 11, ask the children if it is obvious what Winnie will do to solve the problem. Did they guess what she might do from the perspective of the drawing (she is facing the house, her back to us, and Wilbur is looking in the same direction)? What did they think would happen as she waved her wand? If the children had other ideas about what might happen, explore these and discuss if they could have made a better ending for the story. You could also ask the children to come up with their own endings and then vote for the one the class likes the best.

- The final spread shows a picture of Winnie's house again, as it did on the first spread. Tell the children to compare the house and the writing on the first and final spreads and ask them: *Why does the book start and finish with a large picture of Winnie's house?* (A possible answer could be to show readers how the house has changed from the beginning to the end.) Do the children think the change is better? Is it nicer to have more colours? Invite them to suggest what they would have done instead with the colours. For example, would their house be yellow? Would they like a green carpet with pink roses? Encourage children to be creative with their answers, drawing upon their own home décor if desired.

- Consider the final spread and the way Winnie and Wilbur look on it. Do the children think that the two are happier now? What makes them think so? Encourage them to think beyond the obvious (that a good solution has been found to their problem) and look at their expressions. You might like to point out that they both looked happy on the first spread too (so was there any point to Winnie's actions?). Finally, ask them if they think that Winnie and Wilbur will encounter any other problems and, if so, what they might be.

Ask the children, whenever appropriate, to revisit the text to exemplify/support the answers.

Encourage the children to read aloud back to the group when referring back to the text – praise clear, confident and expressive reading.

ASSESSMENT OPPORTUNITIES

The following bank of question prompts provides a quick and easy means of monitoring the children's comprehension skills and understanding of the text. The children's answers to a question must be supported by evidence from the text.

Understanding
- What is Wilbur doing when he comes down from the tree?
- What colours does the wand make on the page when Winnie waves it?
- What colour is the door to her house?
- What is Winnie doing in the final spread?

Inferences:
- Has Wilbur forgiven Winnie for what she did to him?
- Does Winnie like her house better now than before?

Predicting
- Do you think Winnie will trip over Wilbur again?
- Will Winnie use her magic to solve any further problems?

Language, structure and presentation
- Why is the final 'Abracadabra!' in the book so large?
- What does the word 'gleaming' mean and why is it used to describe the colour white?
- Why does the picture in the final spread run across both pages?

Themes and conventions
- Ask the children: *What do you think the message of this story is?* Possible answers could be:
  - never give up when faced with a problem
  - treat others kindly and help them if you have hurt them.

▼ GUIDED READING RECORD

Year		Term	
Group		Reading target	

Date	Text	Objectives	Names	Comments

Notes

▟ SCHOLASTIC
READ & RESPOND
Bringing the best books to life in the classroom

BOOK:

....
....

....
....
....
....
....
....
....
....
....
....

▟ SCHOLASTIC
READ & RESPOND
Bringing the best books to life in the classroom

BOOK:

....
....

....
....
....
....
....
....
....
....
....
....

READ & RESPOND

Bringing the best books to life in the classroom

Plan with confidence

The Planning Guide provides a teaching structure for Years 1–6.

Boost guided reading time

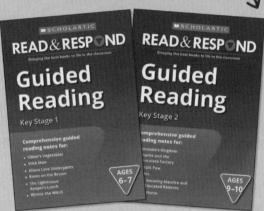

Six guided reading books are available, for Years 1–6.

Teach the best children's books

A huge range of Teacher's Books are available for Years 1–6.

Engage every reader

Children's books are available in sets of 6 and 30.

Order at www.scholastic.co.uk/readandrespond
or call us on 0845 6039091